Sexual Violence

Other Books of Related Interest:

At Issue Series

Date Rape

Current Controversies Series

Family Violence

Human Trafficking

Introducing Issues with Opposing Viewpoints Series

Human Rights

Issues That Concern You Series

Sexual Harassment

Opposing Viewpoints Series

Gendercide

GLOBALVIEWPOINTS

Sexual Violence

Noah Berlatsky, Book Editor

GREENHAVEN PRESS
A part of Gale, Cengage Learning

GALE
CENGAGE Learning·

Farmington Hills, Mich • San Francisco • New York • Waterville, Maine
Meriden, Conn • Mason, Ohio • Chicago

Elizabeth Des Chenes, *Director, Content Strategy*
Cynthia Sanner, *Publisher*
Douglas Dentino, *Manager, New Product*

© 2014 Greenhaven Press, a part of Gale, Cengage Learning

WCN: 01-100-101

Gale and Greenhaven Press are registered trademarks used herein under license.

For more information, contact:
Greenhaven Press
27500 Drake Rd.
Farmington Hills, MI 48331-3535
Or you can visit our Internet site at gale.cengage.com

Articles in Greenhaven Press anthologies are often edited for length to meet page require-ments. In addition, original titles of these works are changed to clearly present the main thesis and to explicitly indicate the author's opinion. Every effort is made to ensure that Greenhaven Press accurately reflects the original intent of the authors. Every effort has been made to trace the owners of copyrighted material.

Cover image copyright © Sharron Ward/ Demotix/Corbis.

LIBRARY OF CONGRESS CATALOGING-IN-PUBLICATION DATA

Sexual violence / Noah Berlatsky, book editor.
    pages cm. -- (Global viewpoints)
    Includes bibliographical references and index.
    ISBN 978-0-7377-6914-2 (hardcover) -- ISBN 978-0-7377-6915-9 (pbk.)
    1. Rape--Case studies. 2. Sex crimes--Case studies. I. Berlatsky, Noah, editor of compilation.
    HV6558.S497 2014
    364.15'3--dc23

                                                              2013036317

Printed in Mexico
1 2 3 4 5 6 7 18 17 16 15 14

Contents

Chapter 1: Sexual Violence and Women

Chapter 2: Sexual Violence and Children

The Supreme Court of South Africa reduced the sentence of a man who raped his daughter on the grounds that he did not use violence. This judgment misunderstands the nature of incest and puts other children at risk.

Chapter 3: Sexual Violence and Migration

Chapter 4: Sexual Violence and Political Violence

Foreword

> "*The problems of all of humanity can only be solved by all of humanity.*"
> —*Swiss author Friedrich Dürrenmatt*

Global interdependence has become an undeniable reality. Mass media and technology have increased worldwide access to information and created a society of global citizens. Understanding and navigating this global community is a challenge, requiring a high degree of information literacy and a new level of learning sophistication.

Building on the success of its flagship series, Opposing Viewpoints, Greenhaven Press has created the Global Viewpoints series to examine a broad range of current, often controversial topics of worldwide importance from a variety of international perspectives. Providing students and other readers with the information they need to explore global connections and think critically about worldwide implications, each Global Viewpoints volume offers a panoramic view of a topic of widespread significance.

Drugs, famine, immigration—a broad, international treatment is essential to do justice to social, environmental, health, and political issues such as these. Junior high, high school, and early college students, as well as general readers, can all use Global Viewpoints anthologies to discern the complexities relating to each issue. Readers will be able to examine unique national perspectives while, at the same time, appreciating the interconnectedness that global priorities bring to all nations and cultures.

Material in each volume is selected from a diverse range of sources, including journals, magazines, newspapers, nonfiction books, speeches, government documents, pamphlets, organization newsletters, and position papers. Global Viewpoints is truly global, with material drawn primarily from international sources available in English and secondarily from US sources with extensive international coverage.

Features of each volume in the Global Viewpoints series include:

- An **annotated table of contents** that provides a brief summary of each essay in the volume, including the name of the country or area covered in the essay.

- An **introduction** specific to the volume topic.

- A **world map** to help readers locate the countries or areas covered in the essays.

- For each viewpoint, an **introduction** that contains notes about the author and source of the viewpoint explains why material from the specific country is being presented, summarizes the main points of the viewpoint, and offers three **guided reading questions** to aid in understanding and comprehension.

- **For further discussion** questions that promote critical thinking by asking the reader to compare and contrast aspects of the viewpoints or draw conclusions about perspectives and arguments.

- A worldwide list of **organizations to contact** for readers seeking additional information.

- A **periodical bibliography** for each chapter and a **bibliography of books** on the volume topic to aid in further research.

- A comprehensive **subject index** to offer access to people, places, events, and subjects cited in the text, with the countries covered in the viewpoints highlighted.

Global Viewpoints is designed for a broad spectrum of readers who want to learn more about current events, history, political science, government, international relations, economics, environmental science, world cultures, and sociology—students doing research for class assignments or debates, teachers and faculty seeking to supplement course materials, and others wanting to understand current issues better. By presenting how people in various countries perceive the root causes, current consequences, and proposed solutions to worldwide challenges, Global Viewpoints volumes offer readers opportunities to enhance their global awareness and their knowledge of cultures worldwide.

Introduction

> *"Violence fuels HIV because it disempow-
> ers women and takes away their right to
> decide when or with whom to have sex.
> Violence against women prevents us
> from getting to zero new HIV infections,
> it prevents us from achieving zero dis-
> crimination and it prevents us from get-
> ting to zero AIDS-related deaths."*
>
> *—Michel Sidibé,
> executive director of UNAIDS,
> Skoll World Forum, 2013*

Worldwide, there is a strong link between sexual violence and infection with the sexually transmissible diseases HIV and AIDS. Women or men may be exposed to HIV during rape, and studies show increased risk of HIV among rape survivors. If a rapist is infected with HIV, the victim may also become infected. Additionally, abrasions or tears during a rape can make it easier for the virus to enter the bloodstream, thus increasing the risk of infection. Anal rape, of men or women, is especially likely to lead to infection.

Violence increases the risk of HIV infection in other ways as well. Individuals subjected to sexual violence as children are more likely to be HIV positive and are also more likely to engage in high-risk behaviors later in life. Women who are in relationships where they suffer abuse are less able to protect themselves from infection. They may be unable to negotiate with their partners for condom use, and they may be unable to refuse unwanted sex. This is particularly dangerous since "physically violent men are more likely to have HIV and to impose risky sexual practices on their partners," according to a post on Sexual Violence and HIV at the Sexual Violence Research Initiative website.

Not only can violence increase HIV exposure, but HIV exposure can increase violence. Revealing HIV/AIDS status can lead to discrimination and abuse. A full 16 percent of men and 14 percent of women in the 15–19 age range said they would not share an HIV diagnosis with their family in a 2004 study in South Africa. HIV sufferers' fears are well warranted; studies in the developing world show that between 3.5 percent to 23 percent of those who disclose their HIV status may face violence, according to a July 2012 report by the United Nations (UN) Trust Fund to End Violence Against Women. The refusal to reveal HIV status because of fear of violence can, in turn, lead to the further spread of the disease to uninformed partners.

Women may be particularly vulnerable to sexual violence and HIV/AIDS in situations of military conflict. In Bosnia-Herzegovina during the 1992–1995 conflict, for example, between 20,000 and 50,000 Muslim women were raped. During the Rwanda genocide, 250,000 women were raped. Such mass acts of sexual violence can cause major increases in HIV. In Rwanda, HIV rates in rural areas jumped from 1 percent before the conflict in 1994 to 11 percent in 1997, according to an informational bulletin by the Global Coalition on Women and AIDS. A full 17 percent of women who survived the genocide had HIV. Another survey found that 67 percent of those who survived rape in Rwanda were HIV positive.

Victims of sexual violence may be able to reduce their chance of contracting HIV if they are able to access prompt medical care. Antiretroviral drugs, or post-exposure prophylaxis (PEP), have been shown to reduce the chances of HIV infection in animal and human trials, according to an article at AVERT. For instance, in one South African study of 480 sexual assault survivors taking PEP, only one became HIV positive.

The evidence is strong enough that many countries have initiated PEP for rape survivors. PEP must be taken within seventy-two hours of exposure, and it must be taken as prescribed for a twenty-eight-day course of treatment if it is to be effective. Unfortunately, PEP can have severe side effects, which sometimes make it difficult for victims to complete treatment. In addition, the stigma associated with HIV and sexual assault means that in some cases victims do not seek out health treatment, or may not be offered PEP if they do seek treatment. For example, victims of male-on-male rape in South Africa face especially high levels of homophobia and stigma, and often do not receive PEP treatments, according to AVERT.

As this suggests, medical treatments are of only limited use if victims are stigmatized or ignored, or if sexual violence is condoned by society at large. According to the July 2012 UN Trust Fund report, reduction of violence and HIV "cannot be sustained if the overall societal context undermines policy and programming." The report argues that advocacy to change attitudes toward victims and those who suffer from HIV is vital. The report points, for example, to the Civil Resource Development and Documentation Centre project in Nigeria that trained HIV-positive women to report violence and follow through with police, health care workers, and legal aid providers. The program also encouraged the women to work as advocates themselves, teaching others in their community.

The UN Trust Fund report also pointed to the importance of media campaigns in changing attitudes and empowering women. For instance, a radio program in Nepal called *VOICES* focused specifically on the stories of women living with violence and HIV. The UN Trust Fund report quotes one Nepalese woman, Sharda Devi Poudel, who said that her husband "never asked me whether I wanted [sex] or not, everything happened per his wish or desire." She did not see this as violence until she listened to *VOICES* and discussed the program with other listeners. She also said that listening to the program made her husband begin to alter his behavior.

Public education through the media, then, can change attitudes and reduce sexual violence—and by doing so, help reduce HIV transmission and infection.

HIV is but one aspect of the worldwide problem of sexual violence. The rest of this book examines other risks and consequences of sexual violence, in chapters titled "Sexual Violence and Women," "Sexual Violence and Children," "Sexual Violence and Migration," and "Sexual Violence and Political Violence." In each chapter, the viewpoints examine how sexual violence affects people around the globe and how such violence can be confronted and reduced.

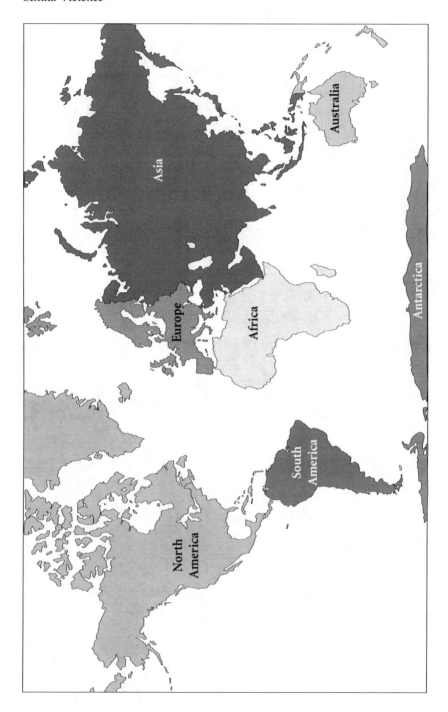

CHAPTER 1

Sexual Violence and Women

The Chinese Government Persecutes Female Victims of Sexual Assault

Zeng Jinyan

Zeng Jinyan is a Chinese blogger and human rights activist. In the following viewpoint, she argues that women who are victims of sexual violence in China receive little aid from authorities and may even be imprisoned or punished. She says that authorities are reluctant to prosecute sexual assaults, especially in cases where the perpetrator is powerful or influential. She says that women who protest may be punished or even imprisoned to keep them from speaking out. She adds that exploitation of young women and institutionalized date rape occur at many official functions while authorities deliberately look the other way.

As you read, consider the following questions:

1. What excuse did the authorities give for not prosecuting Zhou Qin's rape, according to the viewpoint?
2. What does China's criminal law say should be the punishment for rapists?
3. What does the author identify as the essential questions in cases where young female subordinates are exploited or raped by powerful guests at official functions?

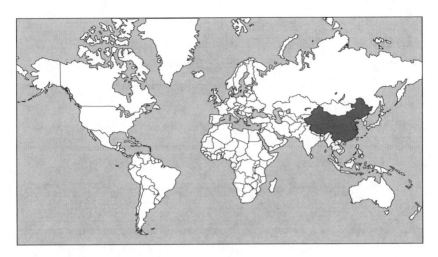

Women who have been raped, sexually violated, or forced to be sex slaves face persecution, not justice, from the authorities in China.

Authorities vs. Victims

Li Hao, a former firefighter and CPC [Communist Party of China] cadre in Luoyang, Henan province was found guilty in a sex dungeon murder case this September [2011]. He had dug dungeons in a local compound, where, over the past two years, he kept a total of six young women aged 16 to 24, who used to work in karaoke clubs or nightclubs. Li killed two of the women and buried them in the dungeons.

The six women were forced to be his sex slaves. Meanwhile, they were forced to be online porn performers and sex workers to earn money for him. Obviously, under such harsh and frightening conditions, being dependent on their kidnapper for survival, some of the women developed serious Stockholm syndrome [that is, the psychological condition in which victims identify with their kidnappers]. One girl escaped while she was forced into sex work outside the dungeon and reported the situation to police.

Southern Metropolis Daily reporter Xu Jiguang was threatened by two local authority officials not to report on this case, on suspicion of "leaking state secrets," when he was investigating the case in Luoyang. Then the surviving four women were put in criminal detention, suspected of participation in Li Hao's murder of the two other women. They are still in custody.

In May, Zhou Qin, a female teacher in Bijie Ashi Middle School, Guizhou province, was raped by Bijie Ashi Town Land and Resources Department director Wang Zhonggui. When she reported this to the police the following day, she was dismissed on the grounds that sex with a condom was "not rape." Before the rape, she had been ordered by the school principal to toast government officials at a banquet and become intoxicated. This is very common in schools nowadays in China— not to mention in government departments and private sectors: Young female staff are "invited" to toast or to "accompany" male guest officials. I have seen this happen myself to former classmates who are now teachers.

The legal system [in China] is biased in favour of power and men on these cases.

Police and other government officials tried very hard to persuade Zhou Qin to settle the rape privately for both sides' sakes, instead of seeking justice. Zhou Qin finally had to disclose her experience on an online forum, asking the public for help. This case stirred up public outrage at the conduct of the police authorities on the Internet. The media started to cover the story in July. Without the pressure of public opinion, Wang Zhonggui would not have been detained two months after committing the rape. Whether Zhou Qin will receive justice in court is still unclear. But, under official pressure, she now refuses interviews with the media.

Relationship Between Perpetrator and Rape Victim in China, 2009

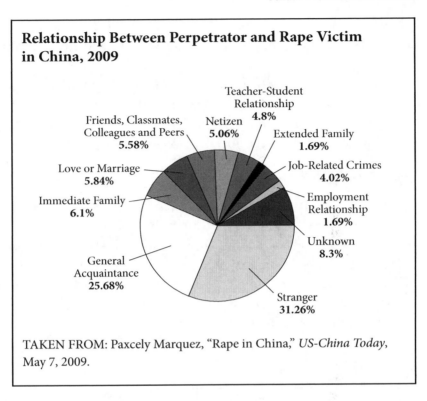

TAKEN FROM: Paxcely Marquez, "Rape in China," *US-China Today*, May 7, 2009.

A similar case happened in Jiangsu province. Wang Yan, a beautiful physical education teacher in Wuxi Professional College of Science and Technology, was often forced by college leaders to attend banquets to please official guests. She was raped twice in January 2010 by a restaurant owner who came from the same hometown as, and was a former student of Zhang Ziwen—the head of her department—and maybe another unknown person too.

This occurred after a banquet organized by Zhang Ziwen. Wang Yan and her family kept silent to protect her reputation. But she broke down and committed suicide on August 8, 2011, days before her scheduled wedding. Zhang Ziwen, who forced Wang Yan to attend banquets and possibly assisted in the rape, and the rapists, whose names are still unknown, are all still free and unfettered. The public had no knowledge of this until her fiancé posted the case on an online forum, which led to media reports.

Indeed, according to article 236 in the Criminal Law of the People's Republic of China, those guilty of rape should be sentenced to three to ten years in jail. But the legal system is biased in favour of power and men on these cases.

The Vulnerability of Sex Workers

In the first case, the kidnapper, Li Hao, is a CPC member, a party cadre, and the victims are probably sex workers whose business is not protected by Chinese law. This illegal status puts sex workers in an extraordinarily vulnerable situation. When their rights are violated, it can even be better for them to remain silent—because, if they speak out, the legal system will punish them before the violator has been caught. Six women, who all came from local districts, disappeared while they were working.

[The sex dungeon survivors'] urgent need for professional psychological care is not a concern for the authorities.

The first disappearance happened two years ago. But, shockingly, there is no information showing that the police were even aware of the disappearances before the escaped girl's report. Another dungeon sex slavery case happened in 2010 in Wuhan, Hubei province. Two girls were confined in one girl's neighbour's dungeon for almost a year. Every time the girls' families asked police how the investigation was going, they got the same response: "no progress."

Furthermore, the threats made to Xu, the journalist, reveal the deeper reason for the detention of the four surviving women: to keep them away from the public and prevent them from releasing more information on the case—to save face for the CPC and the Luoyang government. Although the survivors are also, in a sense, victims of the sex dungeon killings, their urgent need for professional psychological care is not a concern for the authorities.

Date Rape and Exploitation

Forcing young and beautiful female subordinates to please powerful guests has become a hidden rule across the country. Schools cannot escape this hidden rule. Attractive female staff are presented by their employers to guests as "eye candy" and are obliged to get drunk to please them. Those men who are in higher positions are so ambitious that they see women as the second sex, merely to be used.

[The victims of sexual assault] are still suffering twice.

Many of these cases involve alcohol or date rape drugs, and the sexual assault happens while the victim is at a social occasion. The essential questions are: What is the role of the women's employers and the institutions the women are working for? What do they do when their female subordinates are intoxicated? Are they the real directors of date rape? If indeed they do bear responsibilities for their young female staff, why are none of them brought to justice?

Another ironic, but sadly common phenomenon is that when a victim has reported a sexual assault to police, seeking justice, hoping for the violator to be punished by the law, if the violator is powerful or backed by someone important, the victim will be pressured to solve the problem quietly, mostly to save face for the violator and related parties.

It is difficult and frustrating for the victim to insist on justice, as the court usually won't stand for it. Bringing public opinion to bear can force the authorities to change a little, but not enough. Most victims never receive full justice. Some even lose their lives as the price of resistance. They are still suffering twice.

A Gang Rape of a Woman in India Has Provoked a Cultural Conflict

Jason Burke

Jason Burke is a correspondent for the Guardian *and the author of* On the Road to Kandahar: Travels Through Conflict in the Islamic World. *In the following viewpoint, Burke argues that a shocking gang rape in Delhi has created a war over cultural values in India. Burke says that India's modernizing and rapidly changing culture has created great tensions and disagreements over the country's direction. Liberals argue that violence against women is caused by traditional sexism and the low status of women. Conservatives argue that violence is caused by an abandonment of traditional morality.*

As you read, consider the following questions:

1. According to Burke, what has happened to reported cases of rape over the past twenty years?
2. What have village councils in northern India done in response to the rape?
3. What does "Bharat" mean, according to Burke?

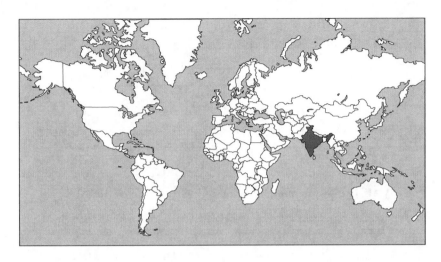

Standing outside the arts faculty of Delhi University, the young men and women drink tea and ready themselves for the protest.

Unsafe for Women

They are from the Akhil Bharatiya Vidyarthi Parishad (ABVP), a student organisation that claims more than 2 million members in India and supports a strongly conservative, nationalist agenda. "We want to make our country and its traditions and morals stronger . . . and through that make our sisters and mothers safe," said Sachin Chandela, 21, who joined the ABVP shortly after the gang rape and murder of a 23-year-old physiotherapy student last month [in December 2012].

The case has provoked outrage and anger, coming against a background of rising violence to women in India. Reported cases of rape have more than doubled in the past 20 years, according to official data, with women being a high proportion of victims of soaring violent crime too.

India's supreme court last week declared Delhi "unsafe" for women. But the gang rape case has also led to a fierce and unprecedented debate on attitudes to women in India. Those who say radical social change is essential to make women safer are clashing with conservatives who say the opposite. Some characterise the confrontation as a "culture war".

Culture War

"There is a conflict and its location is what women can do and not do," said Shoma Chaudhury, managing editor of newsmagazine *Tehelka*. Many conservatives maintain "capitalism and consumerism and growing individualism" have led to "decay in the society". Often "Westernisation" is blamed.

"We must save our culture not just embrace another. These kinds of incidents never happened in India 200 or 300 years ago. . . . Back then there was pride in the soil of our country," said Mamata Yadav, a senior ABVP official. The ABVP has seen a surge in membership since the gang rape on 16 December, said ABVP activist Monika Choudhury, 20. "There are so many coming. They are aware of our ideology and so want to join us. They agree there has been a decline in moral values and this encourages problems [such as rape]."

There are fears the gang rape could lead to further restrictions on women, rather than greater emancipation.

Such views expose cultural and social tensions created by the rapid pace of economic changes in India over recent decades. "Almost as shocking as the Delhi gang rape has been the range of voices that have sounded after it. Patriarchy is chillingly omnipresent and kicking harder than ever before," wrote Sagarika Ghose, a TV journalist and commentator.

There are fears the gang rape could lead to further restrictions on women, rather than greater emancipation. Students at Delhi University spoke of a new pressure from family to avoid public places or "going out". The government of the union territory of Puducherry in the south was set to order all schoolgirls to wear overcoats to "protect them" until a public

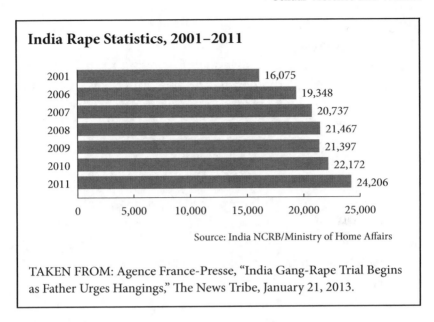

India Rape Statistics, 2001–2011

Year	Number
2001	16,075
2006	19,348
2007	20,737
2008	21,467
2009	21,397
2010	22,172
2011	24,206

Source: India NCRB/Ministry of Home Affairs

TAKEN FROM: Agence France-Presse, "India Gang-Rape Trial Begins as Father Urges Hangings," The News Tribe, January 21, 2013.

outcry forced a U-turn. Delhi police advised women students to "go straight home after college".

Since the rape, a series of village councils in northern India have banned girls from using mobile phones, wearing "decadent" dress or dancing at weddings. "Almost every villager pressed us to ban the mobile phones use by the schoolgirls saying they are . . . dangerous for the society and corrupting local cultures," said Sushma Singh, the local village council head in Matapa, Bihar.

Government Weakness

Such attempts to control women's behaviour are rooted in anxiety and the weakness of the Indian state to protect its citizens, said Reicha Tanwar, of Kurukshetra University, in the northern state of Haryana, where sex ratios are among the most skewed in India and there has been a spate of attacks on women.

"When female foetuses are routinely killed, it is not surprising adult women are also viewed as disposable," Tanwar said. "Women cannot be protected by the state so it is understandable people are looking for other solutions."

Governance is weak and policing patchy in much of rural India, where 70% of the population live. All of the six on trial for the gang rape and murder were born in poor, deeply conservative, lawless rural areas before going to Delhi. But the ABVP and other right-wing organisations, such as the Rashtriya Swayamsevak Sangh (RSS) which claims between 4 and 5 million members, see rural India in a different light.

RSS leader Mohan Bhagwat provoked an outcry when he said recently that rapes were extremely rare in "Bharat", a Sanskrit-origin word which, in this context, evoked a nostalgic vision of a subcontinent supposedly untouched by foreign influences.

"When female foetuses are routinely killed, it is not surprising adult women are also viewed as disposable."

"Bharat means . . . those who kept their original culture. . . . The [recent gang rape] was a heinous crime. Severe punishment and stringent laws are required . . . but also we have to go to the roots. Rape in traditional India was never heard of, certainly not gang rape, it is an imported concept," said Manmohan Vaidya, a top RSS official.

The opposition of a broadly rural "Bharat" and an increasingly urban, globalised "India" touches a deep nerve among many who are disorientated by the pace of change or sense they have much to lose. Many of the increasingly frequent gang rapes have been perpetrated by young, poor, unskilled, often semi-literate men who are low in the tenacious Indian caste system and find little place in new Indian cities, some commentators have argued. Others blame "the values of liberal consumerism".

Shoma Chaudhury, the *Tehelka* managing editor, said the fallout from the most recent incident had "consolidated the conservative view" even if it had inspired a newly "assertive and self-confident expression of feminism". Her magazine recently surveyed male attitudes in India.

"The conservative argument does have purchase. Modernity is seen only as wearing skimpy clothes, not plurality and the assertion of the individual's rights. There is agreement even from conservatives on issues such as women working . . . [the conflict] is all over sexuality," Chaudhury said. The fault lines run deep. Even at Delhi University, students were at odds. "We want to be [economically] developed but without losing our culture," said Neha Singh, 22, an ABVP activist.

Standing under a Delhi police poster saying "Being a woman should not make you feel vulnerable", student Kanika Sharma, 19, disagreed. "It is all about the mentality of the boys. They think because they are men they can do anything. But girls should get equal rights and opportunities. They wear Western clothes but [their] mentality stays the same," she said.

Female Soldiers in the US Military Face Sexual Violence and Rape

Melinda Henneberger

Melinda Henneberger is a political writer for the Washington
Post. *In the following viewpoint, she reports on the problem of
sexual assault in the US military. She says the problem is widespread and that victims have little recourse. The chain of command often protects those accused; few assailants are tried, and
even those who are may end up returning to service. Henneberger
says that Congress has tried to pass laws to correct the problem,
but she concludes that the military still often denies justice to
victims of sexual assault.*

As you read, consider the following questions:

1. According to Henneberger, why was Butcher's assailant
   allowed to go free?

2. How would Klobuchar's bill change the way the military
   handles sexual assault?

3. How does Henneberger say that military victims are
   restricted in comparison to civilians who suffer from
   sexual assault?

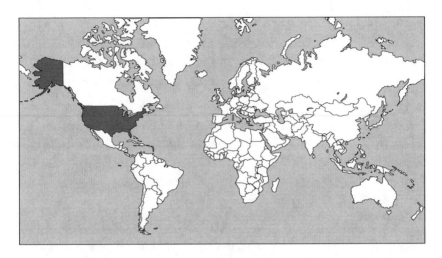

Carla Butcher joined the Navy within days of 9/11 [refer-ring to the September 11, 2001, terrorist attacks on the United States], and soon shipped out for Malta. But during her first hours there, she was raped by a fellow sailor—and spent the remainder of her four years in the service battling both post-traumatic stress disorder [PTSD] and a military justice system that seemed set up to prove she was the guilty party.

All Wrong

Turns out, the man she turned in had already been accused by two other military women, one of whom had been flown home just two weeks before she arrived. And the other, she said, had committed suicide.

Yet under "Don't Ask, Don't Tell,"[1] Butcher couldn't even refute the female defense attorney who got up at the accused sailor's trial and described her as someone "in four-inch heels and tight jeans who wanted it."

"I just had to suck it up," said Butcher, because "if I'd said I don't even sleep with men—I'm a lesbian—I'm the one who

1. A policy at the time under which gays and lesbians in the military could not reveal their sexuality.

would have been out with a dishonorable." In the end, the argument that the sex had been consensual was believed, and the accused went free yet again, just as he'd predicted he would, while her military career was over before it started.

The scale of the problem is a disgrace: The Pentagon itself estimates that there were 19,000 sexual assaults in our military [in 2011].

All wrong, right?

And worse, a hotel ballroom in Washington on Tuesday was packed with women like Butcher, who at 35 is back in college and married to a female minister. Women, that is, of every race, age, background and physical description but with two things in common: All 250 of those brought together by the Service Women's Action Network (SWAN) served our country in uniform.

All, too, had reported being violated in the process—not by the enemy, mind you, but by fellow sailors or soldiers, Americans with whom they were supposed to be fighting the bad guys.

The scale of the problem is a disgrace: The Pentagon itself estimates that there were 19,000 sexual assaults in our military last year [2011]—though only 3,192 of these were officially reported. In a typical year, fewer than 500 cases ever go to trial, and fewer than half of those result in convictions. What's more, a third of those who are convicted, says SWAN's policy director, Greg Jacob, are allowed to stay on in the service.

The first time 25-year-old Joanna Wood, of San Angelo, Texas, reported being raped—also during her first day on her ship, in Norfolk, five years ago—her female superior told her she should confide in a chaplain, because there was nothing she knew to do. Two years later, a coworker and former boyfriend of Wood's, who'd been stalking her, recreated the original attack, which she'd told him about in detail. But that case, too, was dropped, she said, "and I was diagnosed with an anxiety disorder and kicked out" of the Navy in '10, and briefly became homeless.

A few men sexually assaulted in the service were at the SWAN event, too, including David Mair, an Air Force vet from Redding, California, who was raped in Japan way back in 1962—and never told anyone until 2 years ago.

Even then, it took him a while to get in for treatment . . . , he said, though "I literally had a gun to my head." The first doctor to whom he was referred announced that he didn't believe in PTSD, and it was six months before Mair finally saw a therapist.

Why did he fly across the country to discuss an attack that happened 40 years ago? Because he *can* now, he said—though his wife still hopes her family doesn't ever find out, and some friends have tiptoed out of his life since he let them know.

Telling the Truth

Telling the truth about events a lifetime ago and a world away is a relief that those of us who haven't lived through all that he has might not appreciate.

Just telling these horror stories was a big step forward for many in the room. But in recent months, both Congress and the Department of Defense have finally begun to address what the military itself now acknowledges is a serious problem.

Why did he fly across the country to discuss an attack that happened 40 years ago? Because he can *now, he said.*

Senator Amy Klobuchar (D-Minn.), who spoke at the summit, told the crowd that "the idea that an American in uniform who is out there on the front lines serving our country may also suffer the physical and emotional trauma of sexual

An Epidemic

The problems of sexual harassment and sexual assault in the U.S. military are epidemic. Reports of abuse continue to flood in as the problem continues to emerge. Surveys of women in the military tell a story of rampant sexual abuse and harassment by their male counterparts amid concerns that the issues are being minimized or ignored by military leaders. According to a 1997 article, "Did We Say Zero Tolerance?" in *U.S. News & World Report*, "... 18 percent of the Army's women say colleagues have tried to coerce them into having sex and 47 percent say they've received unwanted sexual attention." Similarly, a study in 1995 by the Department of Defense found that 72 percent of women and 63 percent of men had experienced "sexist behavior" and that 47 percent of women and 30 percent of men received "unwanted sexual attention."

T.S. Nelson,
For Love of Country: Confronting Rape
and Sexual Harassment in the U.S. Military.
New York: Routledge, 2002, p. 15.

assault is simply unacceptable, and they shouldn't have to fight to receive care or pursue justice" on top of it.

Klobuchar got every one of the 17 female senators to sign on to a bill to require every branch of the service to start keeping records of such cases for 50 years. Reports had previously been tossed after between one and 5 years, seriously compromising cases against repeat offenders and making it harder for victims to get medical treatment years later, for events there were often no records of.

That legislation was part of the defense reauthorization [President Barack] Obama signed into law in December.

"Given the increasing number of women coming in" to the military "they *have* to deal with it," Klobuchar told me in the hallway after she spoke. And they have to start catching up to changes civilian courts made decades ago.

Justice remains "nearly impossible" to come by.

The Department of Defense does seem to be scrambling to do that. "We are taking this seriously," said spokeswoman Cynthia Smith, establishing a special victims unit in every service branch, improving training for prosecutors and investigators, and making it easier for victims to get transferred away from the accused.

Just today, a letter went out to every service member emphasizing that the military is on the case now.

No Justice

Yet they still have a painfully long way to go. Justice remains "nearly impossible" to come by, says SWAN executive director Anu Bhagwati, because of the likelihood of retaliation within the chain of command. "There's still no deterrent to sexual assault in the military," and no access to the kind of civil remedies that civilian victims can pursue, because service members can't sue for damages.

Mair, who was attacked in Japan all those years ago, said what he wants to tell every single young recruit is "to be aware and to be cautious. I wouldn't want them to be afraid to make friends," he said. "But there are predators" among the good guys, "and you have to know how they operate."

To Reduce Rape of Women in South Africa, Male Attitudes Must Change

Dominic Farrell

Dominic Farrell works for the United Kingdom Department for International Development. In the following viewpoint, he says that rape and domestic battery of women are serious and endemic problems in South Africa. To combat this, he says, male attitudes must be changed. Farrell points to several programs that have tried to change men's attitudes and says that they have had some success. Government educational programs have also been helpful. He concludes that change is difficult, but says that continued efforts can reduce sexual violence in South Africa.

As you read, consider the following questions:

1. What evidence does Farrell provide that Stepping Stones was effective in reducing sexual violence?
2. According to Farrell, what is transactional sex?
3. Besides changing preconceived notions of masculinity, what steps does Farrell say South Africa has to take to reduce sexual violence?

Dominic Farrell, "Sexual Violence: Changing Male Attitudes in South Africa," Think Africa Press, June 14, 2011. Reproduced with permission.

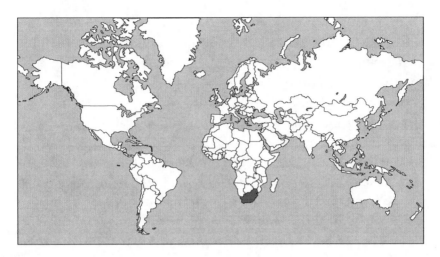

The role of masculinity in gender relations has been the target of gender equality organisations for more than a decade in South Africa. And in the country's twin epidemics of gender violence and HIV/AIDS—South Africa has the highest number of people with HIV/AIDS in the world, while a girl born in the country has a higher chance of being raped than of finishing secondary school—the role of male attitudes is of particular importance.

> *A girl born in [South Africa] has a higher chance of being raped than of finishing secondary school.*

Men as Partners

Two South African civil society organisations, Stepping Stones and Men as Partners (MAP), have made men the focus of their campaigns in the fight against gender violence and HIV/AIDS. The success of these projects suggests that targeting the transformation of men's attitudes is a worthy investment. MAP activist Dumisani Rebombo captures the current state of gender relations and the possibility of transformation: "Power is enjoyable, I guess. I accepted the status quo. Being introduced to gender education made me stop and start thinking and feeling."

By encouraging men to reassess their position in gender relations, organisations like Stepping Stones and Men as Partners can bring new weapons to the fight against sexual violence and the HIV epidemic. Both organisations use a series of workshops which bring gender issues to the wider community. To encourage gender equality, it is important that women are able to communicate their position without fear of intimidation. The workshops seek to make men assess the impact of their actions and assumptions. Men as Partners offers reinforcement in the form of community action teams composed of local men in an effort to permanently embed the progress made in the workshops.

Mixed Results

A study conducted by the Medical Research Council (MRC) in the Eastern Cape demonstrates the positive impact of these programmes. Stepping Stones was shown to have reduced the perpetration of physical and sexual intimate partner violence (IPV) slightly after 12 months, and significantly after 24 months. There were similar decreases in rape, number of sexual partners and alcohol and drug abuse.

Surprisingly, however, an unexpected rise was found in instances of transactional sex, that is sex that is given in return for some form of reward, often money or gifts. Transactional sex extends far beyond the business of prostitution. The vast majority of those engaged in transactional sex do not regard themselves as sex workers.

Studies conducted by the director of the MRC Gender & Health Research Unit in Pretoria, Rachel Jewkes, and Emory University's Kristin Dunkle show that 21.1% of young pregnant women reported offering sex for money—it is likely that there are more women who engage in such relationships. A

2011 study by the MRC in the Western Cape suggests women are not always passive victims of transactional sex, although once 'initiated' there is little doubt that men take control. Sexual exploitation, risk taking and low condom use are all problems inherent to transactional sex, while 85.9% of the women in the study reported intimate partner violence: Aggressive forms of masculinity emerge, to the detriment of the woman.

The Ekukhanyeni Tribal Authority revealed that prior to the workshop, 63% of respondents believed it was acceptable to beat their partners. Following the workshop, 83% believed that it was not acceptable.

The reaction of one respondent reveals the fear that permeates such transactional relationships: "He won't [let her go without having sex with him], he will never, he won't just give it to her. He will drag her then put her in his car and sort her out, rape and then kill her." Masculine notions of sexual conquest ride roughshod over the rights to health and safety of women. Financial and material needs result in an explicit power imbalance in gender relations. Rape and IPV are precipitated by expectations of sex for financial outlay that are frustrated. The needs of the woman are subjected to the desires and needs of the man.

This state of affairs is not just confined to transactional sex. A quarter of South African men have admitted to raping or attempting to rape women, while partner violence forms a part of life for many South African women. Transactional sex degrades and devalues women. And in societies where the status of women is such, rates of rape and IPV are high.

Changing masculine conceptions of women is crucial if gender equality is to be secured in South Africa. Stepping Stones and Men as Partners are not the only organisations to recognise this. The One Man Can Campaign (OMC) conducted by Sonke [Gender Justice Network] has been implemented in eight of South Africa's nine provinces. Workshops, community action teams and digital media target individuals within urban and rural communities, while the campaign also draws on a wide range of other organisations to pressure the government to intervene in the epidemic of gender violence.

The effectiveness of Sonke has been proven in a number of reviews and reports. The Centre for Aids, Development, Research and Evaluation reported that OMC campaigns had a high impact on behaviour, to the extent that participants were passionate about addressing gender issues. The Ekukhanyeni Tribal Authority revealed that prior to the workshop, 63% of the respondents believed it was acceptable to beat their partners. Following the workshop, 83% believed that it was not acceptable.

The View from Government

The importance of tackling the epidemic of gender violence has not escaped government attention either. Widely criticised in the aftermath of his rape trial [in 2005, for which he was acquitted], Jacob Zuma [the president of South Africa] has at least appeared vocal on the government's position on gender issues. A new government department for women, children and persons with disabilities was established upon the formation of his government, with a brief for the 'transformation of gender relations'.

In a statement to the 55th United Nations session [of the Commission] on the Status of Women (UNCSW) in February this year, department minister Lulu Xingwana stated that crimes against women and children were a national priority for the South African government. She highlighted the reintroduction of family violence, child protection and sexual offences units within the police force and the Thuthuzela care programme, which cares for victims of sexual violence, as evidence of government efforts to tackle the epidemic. Upon the launch of the 16 Days of Activism campaign against violence to women and children, the government noted a 4.4% decrease in the total number of sexual offences, but emphasised the large numbers that still suffered abuse. The government appears at least to have realised the scale and intensity of the problem, and has shown that it is prepared to increase its activity.

Challenging preconceived notions of masculinity is but one part of the fight for gender equality.

A Long Road Ahead

So what does the future look like for gender relations in South Africa? Recognition of the extent of the problem by the government has been a crucial step forward. Similarly, acknowledging the central place that prevailing conceptions of masculinity occupy in gender relations is a sign of progress. As the combined work of nongovernmental organisations (NGOs), community-based organisations (CBOs) and the government succeed in changing masculine ideals, pressure for a change in gender relations will increasingly come from communities. Increasing numbers of men are joining the campaign for gender equality.

Challenging preconceived notions of masculinity is but one part of the fight for gender equality. Deficiencies in the legal system remain, which will have to be rectified if increasing numbers of women are to feel able to play a prominent part in achieving gender equality. Strong legal protection will challenge the assumption that perpetrators of gender violence almost always escape unpunished. Economic empowerment will help to reduce the number of women from seeking material gain through transactional sex. The road is long and there are many obstacles. That there is a strong desire on the part of both men and women to overcome such obstacles is, however, clear.

Women in Solomon Islands' Slums Face Endemic Sexual and Physical Violence

Amnesty International

Amnesty International is an international human rights organization. In the following viewpoint, Amnesty International reports that in the slums of the Solomon Islands women face endemic sexual violence. Women often must walk alone for long distances to get water or use toilets, and they are therefore vulnerable to sexual assault. The author says that there is little police presence and that the government often does little to prosecute sexual assaults or domestic violence. The author concludes by saying that conditions in Solomon Islands' slums are a violation of human rights and must be changed.

As you read, consider the following questions:

1. What did the 2009 survey by the Secretariat of the Pacific Community reveal about sexual violence in the Solomon Islands?

2. According to the viewpoint, why did some lawyers in the public solicitor's office refuse to represent some victims of domestic violence?

Amnesty International, *"Where Is the Dignity in That?": Women in Solomon Islands Slums Denied Sanitation and Safety*, September 2011, pp. 10–15. AI Index: ASA 43/ 001/2011. Reproduced with permission.

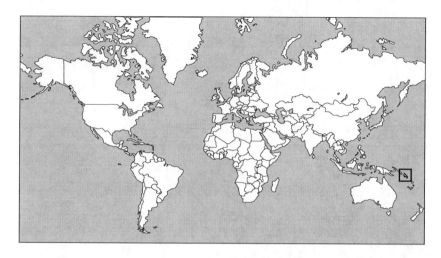

3. What does Amnesty International say is the responsibility of the Solomon Islands under the International Covenant on Economic, Social and Cultural Rights?

Violence against women in Solomon Islands is widespread. A 2009 survey conducted by the Secretariat of the Pacific Community and the government revealed that 64 per cent of women and girls between the ages of 15 and 49 had experienced physical and/or sexual violence from their partners and other family members. The government itself has acknowledged the pervasiveness of violence against women and in 2010, approved a national policy to eliminate violence against women.

It was evidence that there were a large number of sexual assaults happening in slums, many of which went unreported.

Women Attacked and Abused

Women in Honiara's slums face particularly high risks of physical and sexual violence, especially when they are collecting water in the early evening, bathing, or using toilets at night. As described above, they often walk long distances, usually through the bush to get to a water source or to use the toilet. Because there is no electricity, settlements are generally poorly lit at night, with many dark spots which are dangerous for women.

Amnesty International spoke to a number of women who said they were physically or sexually abused by some men outside their household, but were too frightened to make formal complaints to the police for fear of reprisals from their attackers. Women were also afraid to use communal toilets at night, which were relatively far away from their homes, especially if they did not have lanterns or torches.

In August 2010, when Amnesty International met with women's organizations dealing with violence in Honiara, it was evident that there were a large number of sexual assaults happening in slums, many of which went unreported. Women's rights activists in Honiara said that women did not report these assaults for fear of retaliation by their attackers, especially since everyone in the settlement knew each other and women were apprehensive about causing rifts by complaining about their assault.

Violence against women within the family continues to be seen as a private issue and the police and other officials are often reluctant to intervene. In a number of settlements, including Kobito 1, 2, 3 and 4, the existence of a police post in the area has done little to prevent the harassment and assault of women and girls.

Beaten and Raped

Amnesty International interviewed a number of women who had been assaulted while bathing, going to the toilet or collecting water. In August 2010, a 37-year-old woman who lives in Mamanawata settlement told Amnesty International that six months previously she had been severely beaten up and raped by two men in the settlement after relieving herself in the sea:

> The two men were standing by the beach when I finished. I recognized them immediately from their voices. I knew they were drunk because I saw them drinking in the dilapidated house close to the road in the early evening.
>
> They came and one of them grabbed my arm and one closed his hand over my mouth. They held me down and took my clothes off and raped me. They were very violent and I had bruises all over my body. I wanted to die desperately and I was crying and crying thinking of my children. After they raped me, they warned me that if I told anyone they would cut me up. I was so afraid but couldn't do anything. I see them around the settlement but I wouldn't dare tell the police. They're very violent and lawless and will not hesitate to hurt me again.

"I couldn't trust the police because they will not help me. I have to live with this shame for the rest of my life."

An 18-year-old woman from Kobito 4 settlement told Amnesty International about her experience of sexual violence:

> I dropped out of school five years ago because we couldn't afford to pay the fees, uniform and my bus fare to school every day. Since then, I have stayed at home and helped my mother and father with the house chores. We are very poor and my father sells betel nut at the market up the road. Every day I walk to the broken water pipe in Kobiloko to collect water. I walk in the morning for the water to be used in the day and then walk in the afternoon for our evening drinking and cooking water.
>
> About a year ago, while walking to collect water in the afternoon, I was gang-raped by six boys from the nearby settle-

ment. They always drink kwaso by the roadside and when I walked past them, they started calling me to go and say hello to them. I didn't say anything and kept on walking. I was also worried that it was going to get dark soon and I still had a long way to walk to the pipe.

On my way back with the water, I met the same boys up the hill. It had gotten dark and they began to harass me. One of them said that they could carry the water for me. When I said no, he got angry and said that I had insulted him. He demanded that the only way to compensate for that was to have sex with him. I refused and he punched me in the stomach. The others then grabbed me and carried me to the bush where I was raped. They each raped me and then left me there after threatening to kill me and my family. I had a black eye and was sore.

I was so ashamed for being raped. I vowed not to tell my family because it would bring shame to them. I took the water home and didn't tell my family anything. I couldn't trust the police because they will not help me. I have to live with this shame for the rest of my life. I still walk to the pipe to collect water but this time I have a friend or relative that walks with me. I see those boys sometimes but they don't talk to me and look down when I walk past them.

A 23-year-old woman said that she was raped in Adiliwa settlement when she came home late after university classes in September 2008. She had gone for a bath at dusk in a stream about 100m from her home.

"The man came from nowhere," she said. "I was quite shocked! I did not have any undergarments and just had my sarong on. I couldn't scream because he warned me not to scream. It was very easy for him to rape me! *Mifala crae crae nomo!* [I just cried and cried]. I can't believe that it happened to me. . . . I was so stupid to come alone. He was from a neighbouring settlement."

These types of crimes of sexual violence are common, especially for unaccompanied women.

No Privacy

While gender-based violence is endemic in Solomon Islands, women in settlements also face a great deal of indignity in collecting water, going to the toilet, bathing in the river or streams and changing in front of men who are often playing in adjacent fields. In Kobito 2 settlement, for instance, women and children bathed publicly in the same stream where they washed their clothes and cooking and eating utensils.

Women also told Amnesty International that it was sometimes difficult for them to wash themselves properly in the open streams, particularly when they are menstruating, because of the lack of privacy. Such conditions violate women's right to privacy.

"Young men often spy on us and we can hear them laughing and whistling," said a 29-year-old mother of two. "*Mi les long olgeta* [I don't like it when they do that]. I have no choice because it's too heavy to carry the water a long way to my home on the ridge!"

Women in some settlements in Honiara told Amnesty International that not having any toilets to use is embarrassing and demeaning. "When we have heavy rain, our pit toilets are unusable so we have to do it in the open," explained one 32-year-old housewife. "We try and walk to the bush and do it there but we are always wary of men who will come and spy on us. It is easier to do this at night but then we can't walk too far from our homes because we can be harassed and in some cases, assaulted. I wish we had a good, clean and safe toilet with electricity so we can feel much safer."

Failure to Protect Women from Gender-Based Violence

Amnesty International welcomes the government's adoption of a gender policy in March 2010 and its intention to adopt specific legislation to address violence against women. These initiatives, following a 2009 survey, came as a result of lobbying efforts by women's groups and the strong commitment of officials in the Ministry of Women, Youth and Children Affairs.

Not having any toilets to use is embarrassing and demeaning.

In an August 2010 media report, the mayor of Honiara stated that two-thirds of women in Solomon Islands experience violence from their partners during their lifetime. He said that often domestic violence is not reported to the police and that even when suspects are investigated and prosecuted, their cases are given a low priority. He reported that the government is stepping up efforts to combat such violence through legislation, improved law enforcement, and better services for victims.

Amnesty International welcomes such statements; however, Amnesty International's investigations also revealed that some lawyers in the public solicitor's office (PSO) had refused to represent victims of domestic violence seeking a restraining order from the court unless the victim had visible injuries to her body. The Family Support Centre in Honiara told Amnesty International that several battered women from Kobito 2 and 4 who had approached them for assistance were refused representation by the PSO lawyers because they did not have "black eyes and bruises on their bodies".

In other cases, women seeking assistance in obtaining a restraining order after being threatened by their partners with a knife had been asked to come back to the PSO several days later because their complaint was not seen as important enough or requiring urgent attention due to the absence of physical injuries. In such circumstances, women fearful of returning to their homes had sought refuge at the Family Support Centre, who then intervened with the police and the PSO on their behalf.

In a 2008 Australian Agency for International Development (AusAID) report, it was noted that the penal code covers only some forms of domestic violence, that there is no specific crime of domestic violence, and marital rape is not a criminal offence. To Amnesty International's knowledge, the penal code has not yet been amended to criminalize these offences although a legislative reform task force has been set up to reform laws to address domestic violence.

State Negligence

The Ministry of Lands, Housing and Survey is responsible for the planning and administration of all land in Solomon Islands. However, Honiara's slums fall within the jurisdiction of the Honiara City Council and some of the settlements have spilled over to land belonging to the Guadalcanal provincial government.

> *There is no specific crime of domestic violence, and marital rape is not a criminal offence.*

In August 2010, Amnesty International held meetings with senior representatives of the Honiara City Council about the situation in Honiara's slums. However, both national and local government officials said that the solution to overcrowding and lack of basic infrastructure in slums was for residents to return to their villages. The officials interviewed stated that the problems faced by people in slums were the fault of the people concerned and not that of the government.

"It is the responsibility of the government to enforce the law and evict those who have settled on our land," said a Guadalcanal provincial government official. "If we don't do this, then we can have a repeat of the [ethnic] tension."

As a state party to the International Covenant on Economic, Social and Cultural Rights, Solomon Islands must take steps to ensure that each person has access to sufficient, safe, physically accessible and affordable water, especially for personal and domestic uses. It must also ensure that everyone, without discrimination, has physical and affordable access to sanitation which is hygienic and safe. The government is required to ensure provision of security of tenure and access to essential services.

In discussions with Amnesty International in August 2010, one of the senior planners in the Honiara town council stated that it was very difficult for the council to enforce any of its bylaws relating to water and sanitation in slums. He said that a building code has been in draft form for a long time but that there has been no agreement to adopt it. He also told Amnesty International that the council did not know where to start in addressing the challenges in slums and faced difficulties because of the increase in the population of the settlements. There was an attempt by the government to introduce a credit scheme in 2007 so people could borrow money to build their houses. However, this has not taken effect.

Every day, they must struggle alone to provide clean water for themselves and their families. In doing so, they are targeted for harassment, sexual violence, and rape.

Solomon Islands Water Authority (SIWA), which is owned by the government, is responsible for providing water to communities throughout Solomon Islands, including to the people of Honiara. However SIWA has not addressed the problems of water and sanitation in slums. Residents have to pay SIWA connection fees to set up a piped water connection to their community, but these fees are usually too expensive for them.

The health department sends out health inspectors to the settlements to raise awareness on health issues and the use of water and sanitation. But as one inspector explained, little can be achieved without adequate water and sanitation facilities.

"No one knows what to do," he said. "We talk to the people [residents] about health and sanitation but we know that they can't do anything because there is no water, they have no money to build better toilets. Diarrhoea is widespread. It is so sad to be helpless and without hope."

Deprived of one of the most basic requirements for survival—an accessible source of clean water and safe toilets—residents in Honiara's slums are condemned to live in squalid conditions.

Women and girls bear a disproportionate burden in this tragedy, which affects their ability to live in safety and dignity. Every day, they must struggle alone to provide clean water for themselves and their families. In doing so, they are targeted for harassment, sexual violence, and rape. Even when they go to the toilet or bathe, they risk being harassed or attacked.

It is an unsustainable situation which needs urgent attention from the authorities. The response so far has ranged from outright refusal to acknowledge a problem to toothless gestures. It is time for the government to step up to its responsibilities and restore some hope to these neglected communities.

Worldwide, Children of Rape and Their Mothers Face Difficult Challenges

Andrew Solomon

Andrew Solomon is a writer on politics, culture, and psychology who has written for the New Yorker, *the* New York Times, *and other publications. In the following viewpoint, Solomon discusses the plight of women who have been raped and become pregnant. He says that such women face severe psychological trauma. He argues that it is important that women who have been raped have the choice to abort the baby or to keep it. Since rape is an abusive loss of control, having control over her own body is extremely important for the victim. He says that mothers who do bear children of rape face serious psychological hurdles and may have trouble loving or caring for the child.*

As you read, consider the following questions:

1. What was Augustine's attitude toward rape?
2. What did Susan Brownmiller say about rape in her 1975 book *Against Our Will: Men, Women and Rape*?
3. What did his final interviewee ask Solomon?

Writing in the *American Journal of Preventive Medicine,* Dr. Felicia H. Stewart and Dr. James Trussell have estimated that there are twenty-five thousand rape-related pregnancies each year in the United States. While these numbers make up only a small part of this country's annual three million unwanted pregnancies, the numbers are still extremely high. Nonetheless, the relationship between rape and pregnancy has been a topic of highly politicized debate since long before Todd Akin's[1] comments on "legitimate rape," Paul Ryan's bill with its category of "forcible rape,"[2] and Sharron Angle's suggestion, two years ago, that women pregnant through rape make "a lemon situation into lemonade."[3] There is a veritable war of statistics about rape and pregnancy, and the confusion is exacerbated by the competing agendas of the pro-choice and anti-abortion movements. It has been argued that fear promotes ovulation, and that women who are raped have a ten per cent risk of pregnancy; there are estimates of as little as one per cent. Numbers are also skewed when they are adjusted to include or exclude women not of reproductive age; for sodomy and other forms of rape that cannot cause pregnancy; for rape victims who may be using oral birth control or I.U.D.s [intrauterine devices]; and for women who are raped and become or are pregnant as a result of consensual sex with a husband or partner who is not the rapist, before or after the rape. Women who are being abused on an ongoing basis are particularly likely to conceive in rape. Catharine MacKinnon has written, "Forced pregnancy is familiar, beginning in rape and proceeding through the denial of abortions; this occurred during slavery and still happens to women who cannot afford abortions."

1. Todd Akin was a Republican Senate candidate in 2012. During the campaign, he said that women who experienced "legitimate rape" did not become pregnant.
2. Paul Ryan is an influential U.S. representative; he cosponsored a bill in which the term "forcible rape" was used. Critics said the term sought to suggest some rape was less serious than others.
3. Sharron Angle made her comments while running for the Nevada Senate seat in 2010.

Far from the Tree

I have been researching a book, *Far from the Tree*, that deals in part with women raising children conceived in rape, and have therefore met the living reproof to Akin's remark. Life for these children may be extremely difficult. One of the few groups founded to address this population, Stigma Inc., took as its motto, "Rape survivors are the victims . . . their children are the forgotten victims."

And yet there's a lot of history behind their experience, and that of their mothers. Augustine [an early Christian saint and theologian] saw a noble purpose in rape; while promising women that "savage lust perpetuated against them will be punished," he also praises rape for keeping women humble, letting them know "whether previously they were arrogant with regard to their virginity or over-fond of praise, or whether they would have become proud had they not suffered violation." The Roman physician Galen claimed that women could not conceive in rape—could not, in fact, conceive without an orgasm based in pleasure and consent. Classical mythology is full of rape, usually seen as a positive event for the rapist, who is often a god; Zeus so took Europa and Leda; Dionysus raped Aura; Poseidon, Aethra; Apollo, Evadne. It is noteworthy that every one of these rapes produces children. The rape of a vestal virgin by Mars produced Romulus and Remus, who founded Rome. Romulus organized the rape of the Sabine women to populate his new city. In much later civilizations, the rape of the Sabines was considered a noble story; in the Renaissance, it often graced marriage chests. The hostility such children inspired due to their origins has also long been acknowledged. In both the ancient and the medieval world, women who bore children conceived in rape were permitted to let them die of exposure—although in medieval Europe a few weeks' penance was deemed necessary for doing so.

A Troubled History

Historically, rape has been seen less as a violation of a woman than as a theft from a man to whom that woman belonged, either her husband or her father, who suffered an economic loss (a woman's marriageability spoiled) and an insult to his honor. There was also the problem of bastard children, who were considered a social burden; the Athenian state, for example, was primarily occupied with protecting bloodlines, and so treated rape and adultery the same way. Hammurabi's code describes rape victims as adulterers; English law of the seventeenth century takes a similar position. In Puritan Massachusetts, any woman pregnant through rape was prosecuted for fornication. In the nineteenth century, the American courts remained biased toward protecting men who might be falsely accused. In order to prove that an encounter was a rape, the woman had to demonstrate that she had resisted and been overcome; she usually had to show bodily harm as evidence of her struggle; and she had somehow to prove that the man had ejaculated inside her.

"Rape survivors are the victims . . . their children are the forgotten victims."

In the early and mid-twentieth century, rape remained underreported because women feared adverse consequences if they spoke out about what had happened to them. In 1938, Dr. Aleck Bourne was put on trial in England for performing an abortion on a fourteen-year-old rape victim, and his acquittal reflected a populist movement to liberalize abortion, especially for rape victims. The trial was widely covered in the U.S. and led to open debate about the validity of abortion; the following year, the first hospital abortion committee in the United States was formed, and by the nineteen fifties these committees were ubiquitous. Although they approved only "therapeutic" abortions, they increasingly accepted the recommendations of psychiatrists who said a woman's mental health was endangered by her pregnancy. Well-connected and well-to-do women could obtain psychiatric diagnoses fairly easily, and so abortions became the province of the privileged. Ordinary rape victims often had to prove that they were nearly deranged. Some were diagnosed as licentious, and had to consent to sterilization to obtain abortions. Here is a typical caseworker report about a woman who had been raped in the postwar, pre-*Roe* era:

> She became a passive object and could not say "no." Here we see a girl who having lost parental love, continues to search for love and her primary motivation became centered in getting her dependent needs met. She took the man's sexual interest as love and an opportunity to be loved by somebody.

Historically, rape has been seen less as a violation of a woman than as a theft from a man to whom that woman belonged.

That is to say, mentally stable people are not the kind who get raped. The emerging field of psychoanalysis did not help matters. Though [Sigmund] Freud himself wrote little about rape, Freudians in the early and mid-twentieth century saw the rapist as someone suffering a perverse, uncontrolled sexual appetite, who fed into women's natural masochism. This position seemed to exonerate the rapist; in 1971, the psychoanalyst Menachem Amir called rape a "victim-motivated crime." A rapist was the embodiment of virility, while those who were raped were utterly abject; the aggression was deplored less than the disenfranchisement was pitied.

Appalled at such positions, feminists of the nineteen seventies began the reclassification of rape as an act of violence and aggression rather than of sexuality. Susan Brownmiller's 1975 landmark *Against Our Will: Men, Women and Rape* main-

---

Todd Akin and "Legitimate" Rape

Todd Akin [a former Republican member of Congress from Missouri who ran for a seat in the Senate in 2012] and his supporters try to distance themselves from the rape issue by claiming that "legitimate," or forcible, rape does not lead to pregnancy. According to Akin's pseudoscience, a woman's body "shuts down" and does not allow a pregnancy to occur.

What is ironic about this "shutting down" of a woman's body is that this very argument supports the idea that a rape victim can "self-abort" by not allowing the fertilized egg to implant.

But such an argument of self-abortion, proceeding logically from a flawed premise, is piling insanity on top of insanity.

C. Arthur Ellis Jr. and Leslie E. Ellis, Bible Bullies: How Fundamentalists Got the Good Book So Wrong. *Lutz, FL: Gadfly Publishing, 2013.*

---

tained that rape had very little to do with desire and everything to do with domination. She proposed that rape was a much more frequent occurrence than had previously been acknowledged, that it was not the obscure behavior of a very occasional person with severe mental illness but rather a common result of the power differential between men and women. She also tied the problem of rape to the issues of pregnancy, writing, "Men began to rape women when they discovered that sexual intercourse led to pregnancy."

The Aftermath of Rape

For several of the women I interviewed, the crisis was exacerbated by the question of what rape means, by the idea that some rape is not forcible or legitimate. Men who have gotten away with rape seldom retreat in shame or repentance; they often play out their ghoulish exuberance by claiming their reproductive successes. Among the women I interviewed, such men's bids for custody or visitation rights felt far more like acts of further aggression than expressions of care. Nevertheless, in instances where rape cannot be proven or charges were never filed, the threat of joint custody is real. Many women who cannot cope with prosecuting their assailant are then left without any proof of assault. In a time when DNA evidence can establish biological ties scientifically, this lack of evidence as to the social circumstances of conception can be a serious problem. Stigma Inc. had a posting that read, "The father/rapist is thus deemed ineligible for visitation or custody of the minor child. However, as in the case of rape victims in general, the burden of proof that a rape took place is often placed upon the woman who has suffered the crime. Often it comes down to a 'he said/she said' issue."

Rape is a permanent damage; it leaves not scars but open wounds. As one woman I saw said, "You can abort the child, but not the experience."

The aftermath of rape is always complicated. Many victims are simply in denial that they are pregnant in the first place: A full third of the pregnancies resulting from rape are not discovered until the second trimester. Any delay in detection reduces women's options, especially outside major urban centers, but many women struggle with the speed of the decision; they are still recovering from being raped when they are called on to make up their minds about an abortion. The decision of whether or not to carry through with such a pregnancy is nearly always an ordeal that can lead, no matter which choice is ultimately made, to depression, anxiety, insomnia, and P.T.S.D. [post-traumatic stress disorder]. Rape is a permanent damage; it leaves not scars, but open wounds. As one woman I saw said, "You can abort the child, but not the experience."

An Internal Foreigner

Even women who try to learn their child's blamelessness can find it desperately difficult. The British psychoanalyst Joan Raphael-Leff writes of women bearing children conceived in rape, "The woman feels she has growing inside her part of a hateful or distasteful Other. Unless this feeling can be resolved, the foetus who takes on these characteristics is liable to remain an internal foreigner, barely tolerated or in constant danger of expulsion, and the baby will emerge part-stranger, likely to be ostracized or punished." One rape survivor, in testimony before the Louisiana [State] Senate Committee on Health and Welfare, described her son as "a living, breathing torture mechanism that replayed in my mind over and over the rape." Another woman described having a rape-conceived son as "entrapment beyond description" and felt "the child was cursed from birth"; the child ultimately had severe psychological challenges and was removed from the family by social services concerned about his mental well-being. One of the women I interviewed said, "While most mothers just go with their natural instincts, my instincts are horrifying. It's a constant, conscious effort that my instincts not take over."

Rape Victims Need Choice

The rape exception in abortion law is so much the rule that many women who wish to keep children conceived in rape describe an intense social pressure to abort them, and the pressure to abort can be as sinister as the restriction of access to abortion. There can be no question that, for some women, an abortion would be far more traumatic than having a rape-conceived child. I read the harrowing autobiography of a girl who was put under involuntary anesthesia to have an abortion of the pregnancy that had occurred when her father raped her, so that her parents could keep their reputation intact. It's a horrifying story because the abortion clearly constitutes yet another assault: it is about a lack of choice. But ready access to a safe abortion facility allows a woman who keeps a child conceived in rape to feel that she is making a conscious decision, while having the baby because she has no choice perpetuates the trauma and is bad for the child. Rape is, above all other things, non-volitional for the victim, and the first thing to provide a victim is control. Raped women require unfettered choice in this arena: to abort or to carry to term, and, if they do carry to term, to keep the children so conceived or to give them up for adoption. These women, like the parents of disabled children, are choosing the child over the challenging identity attached to that child. The key word in that sentence is "choosing."

One rape survivor ... described her son as "a living, breathing torture mechanism that replayed in my mind over and over the rape."

One sees the problem abroad, where the Helms Amendment[4] is taken to mean that no agency receiving U.S. funding can mention abortion even to women who have been systematically raped as part of a genocidal campaign. The journalist Helena Smith wrote the story of a woman named Mirveta, who gave birth to a child conceived in rape in Kosovo. Mirveta was twenty years old, and illiterate; her husband had abandoned her because of the pregnancy. "He was a healthy little boy and Mirveta had produced him," Smith writes. "But birth, the fifth in her short lifetime, had not brought joy, only dread. As he was pulled from her loins, as the nurses at Kosovo's British-administered university hospital handed her the baby, as the young Albanian mother took the child, she prepared to

---

4. Named for Senator Jesse Helms and enacted in 1973, the Helms Amendment prohibits U.S. funding of abortion as part of foreign aid.

do the deed. She cradled him to her chest, she looked into her boy's eyes, she stroked his face, and she snapped his neck. They say it was a fairly clean business. Mirveta had used her bare hands. It is said that, in tears, she handed her baby back to the nurses, holding his snapped, limp neck. In Pristina, in her psychiatric detention cell, she has been weeping ever since." The aid worker taking care of Mirveta said, "Who knows? She may have looked into the baby's face and seen the eyes of the Serb who raped her. She is a victim, too. Psychologically raped a second time."

Rape is, above all other things, non-volitional for the victim, and the first thing to provide a victim is control.

In working on my book, I went to Rwanda in 2004 to interview women who had borne children of rape conceived during the genocide. At the end of my interviews, I asked interviewees whether they had any questions for me, in hopes that the reversal would help them to feel less disenfranchised in the microcosmic world of our interview. The questions tended to be the same: How long are you spending in the country? How many people are you interviewing? When will your research be published? Who will read these stories? Why are you interested in me? At the end of my final interview, I asked the woman I was interviewing whether she had any questions. She paused shyly for a moment. "Well," she said, a little hesitantly. "You work in this field of psychology." I nodded. She took a deep breath. "Can you tell me how to love my daughter more?" she asked. "I want to love her so much, and I try my best, but when I look at her I see what happened to me and it interferes." A tear rolled down her cheek, but her tone turned almost fierce, challenging. "Can you tell me how to love my daughter more?" she repeated.

Perhaps Todd Akin has an answer for her.

Periodical and Internet Sources Bibliography

The following articles have been selected to supplement the diverse views presented in this chapter.

BBC News	"China Protests Citizen's Rape in India," February 8, 2013.
Maria Hengeveld	"South Africa Finally Wakes Up to Sexual Violence," *Guardian*, February 15, 2013.
Robert C. Koehler	"Rape Culture and the US Military," Truthout, November 15, 2012. http://truth-out.org /buzzflash/commentary/item/17645-rape -culture-and-the-us-military.
Dean Nelson	"Rape and Murder of Three Young Sisters Renews Public Anger in India," *Sydney Morning Herald*, February 21, 2013.
Sutirtho Patranobis	"Stricter Laws on Rape in China but Prejudices Against Women Exist," *Hutong Cat*, January 2, 2013. http://blogs.hindustantimes.com /hutong-cat/2013/01/02/stricter-laws-on -rape-in-china-but-prejudices-against-women -exist/.
Radio Australia	"Solomon Islands Worst Country for Sexual Violence Against Women—World Bank," March 26, 2012.
Solomon Star	"Marital Rape Removed from Country's Law," November 1, 2012.
Heather Timmons, Niharika Mandhana, and Sruthi Gottipati	"Six Charged with Murder in India After Rape Victim's Death," *New York Times*, December 29, 2012.
World Health Organization	"Violence Against Women," October 2013. http://www.who.int/mediacentre/factsheets /fs239/en/.

GLOBAL VIEWPOINTS

CHAPTER 2

Sexual Violence and Children

Sexual Violence Against Afghani Children Is Commonplace

Murray Brewster

Murray Brewster is a Canadian journalist and the author of The Savage War: The Untold Battles of Afghanistan. *In the following viewpoint, he says that sexual abuse of young boys and illegal marriage of underage girls are common and endemic in Afghanistan. He says Canadian officials are reluctant to acknowledge the problem. Canadian spokespeople have pointed to their programs for schooling and child education as a sign of their support for Afghani children, but Brewster says that many of these efforts are undermined by poor security in Afghanistan.*

As you read, consider the following questions:

1. What statistics does Brewster cite to show the abysmal treatment of young Afghan girls?
2. What is "baad" and how is the practice changing, according to Brewster?
3. What statistics does Brewster use to highlight the security concerns for schools in Afghanistan?

Murray Brewster, "Sexual Violence Against Children Common in Afghanistan: Report," RAWA, June 7, 2009. Reproduced with permission.

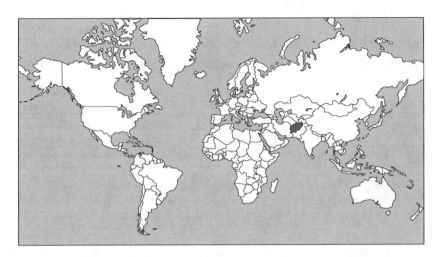

The trafficking and sexual exploitation of children in Afghanistan is a growing concern, Canada's Foreign Affairs Department was told in a confidential human rights report prepared by senior officials.

Abuse Is Common

The illegal marriage of underage girls and the sexual abuse of young boys are commonplace, warned the Afghanistan human rights report obtained by the Canadian Press under access-to-information laws.

"Sexual violence is commonly reported but remains difficult to verify," said the partially censored review, written last summer [in 2008].

"Trafficking in children is a problem in Afghanistan and the majority of the children trafficked are boys who are trafficked for the purpose of sexual exploitation and forced labour."

The red flag was penned around the same time Canadian military police began investigating public complaints that soldiers and their commanders had turned a blind eye to the rape of young boys by Afghan troops and police at a forward operating base. The military's National Investigative Unit has been unable to verify the allegations.

A second, procedural investigation by the Canadian military continues and is expected to table its findings within weeks.

The Foreign Affairs analysis cited a Geneva-based human rights group in its warning about children. "According to the International Organization for Migration, trafficking in children is a problem in Afghanistan and the majority of the children trafficked are boys who are trafficked for the purpose of sexual exploitation and forced labour," said the report.

The NDP [New Democratic Party] foreign affairs critic, Paul Dewar, said the assessment is disturbing, especially in light of the abuse allegations, which he claimed the Canadian military isn't eager to substantiate.

"The Afghans know this is going on; they're not stupid," Dewar said. "It's a case of 'see no evil; hear no evil; speak no evil' and therefore there's no evil."

"There have been many claims that abuse is going on, but I suppose if you don't acknowledge there's actually problems, then there are no problems." The treatment of young girls is just as abysmal. Figures indicated 57 per cent of Afghan marriages involved girls under the legal age of 16. Many of those unions are arranged marriages, where the girls are sometimes used to pay off family debts and those who disobey become the victims of so-called honour killings.

The report tried to cast a hopeful note by recognizing that the Afghan practice of "baad" had begun to decline. "The use of women as compensation in dispute resolution, has decreased due to awareness campaigns by the (Afghan) government and human rights organizations."

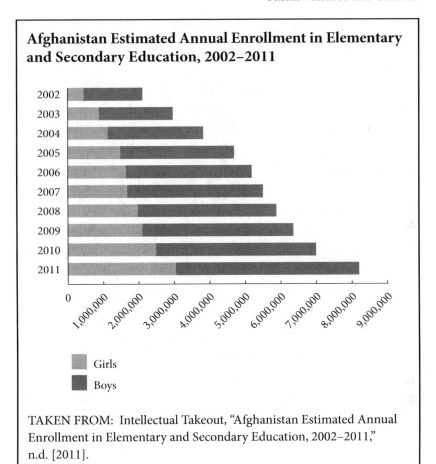

Afghanistan Estimated Annual Enrollment in Elementary and Secondary Education, 2002–2011

TAKEN FROM: Intellectual Takeout, "Afghanistan Estimated Annual Enrollment in Elementary and Secondary Education, 2002–2011," n.d. [2011].

Canada's Support for Afghan Children

A Foreign Affairs official said Ottawa has invested a lot of time and money to improve the lives of Afghan children, pointing to a series of initiatives, including the campaign to eradicate polio.

"Canada's support for children and youth in Afghanistan is demonstrated in its support for programming in education, child and maternal health, and through our commitment to improve access to basic service and provide increased economic opportunities for Kandaharis," said Laurent Morel-à-l'Huissier, in an email note.

Morel-à-l'Huissier pointed to the country's falling infant mortality rate as sign of progress and said the school construction "is a major reason why so many boys and girls are in school today, more than at any time in Afghanistan's history."

More than six million children are enrolled in classes, with roughly 35 per cent of them girls—a vast improvement from the days of the brutal [radical Islamist] Taliban regime [of the 1990s], under which girls were barred from attending school.

But behind those cheery, often-quoted statistics is the reality that "half of all school-age children do not attend school, including the majority of school-age girls," said the human rights report.

Canada has committed to expand and repair 50 schools in Kandahar as one of its benchmarks to be accomplished by the time the forces end their combat mission in 2011. According to the latest progress report, five of those schools are completed with another 25 in the planning or construction stage. But officials are not eager to address the question of whether those buildings will ever be used because, as the report noted, security for the education sector remains "a concern."

But behind these cheery, often-quoted statistics is the reality that "half of all school-age children do not attend school, including the majority of school-age girls."

The Afghan education ministry has reported that 538 schools were closed as of June 2008, including 58 per cent of the schools in Kandahar province, mostly outside the provincial capital.

In the 10 months between May 2007 and February 2008, 147 teachers and students were killed (57 in a November 2007 suicide bomb attack) and 98 schools were burned. Between March and June 2008, 14 schools were burned and 14 students killed.

Trade minister Stockwell Day, who's in charge of the Afghanistan file, said school security is a "very high concern" and Canadian troops work with Afghans daily to ease the threats.

Child Rape Is a Serious Problem in Sri Lanka

Amantha Perera

Amantha Perera is a journalist and foreign correspondent based in Colombo, Sri Lanka. In the following viewpoint, Perera argues that there is a serious problem with child sexual abuse and child rape in Sri Lanka. He says that there are numerous incidents of child rape, but that they are often covered up or silenced, perhaps because of Sri Lankans' discomfort with discussing sexuality. He says that some activists have been trying to highlight the issue, and he concludes that more must be done to address the sexual violence.

As you read, consider the following questions:

1. What unusual step did Diarietou Gaye take to confront sexual violence in Sri Lanka?
2. What ended in northern Sri Lanka in May 2009, according to Perera?
3. According to surveys, what do Sri Lankans believe the punishment for child rape should be?

It was the ghostly silence that struck him hardest as he walked through the Colombo suburb of Kirulapone the day after the lifeless body of a six-year-old girl had been discovered floating in a filthy canal, Kumar de Silva, a well-known local media personality, told IPS [Inter Press Service].

Amantha Perera, "Breaking the Ghostly Silence on Rape," IPS, July 30, 2012. Reproduced with permission.

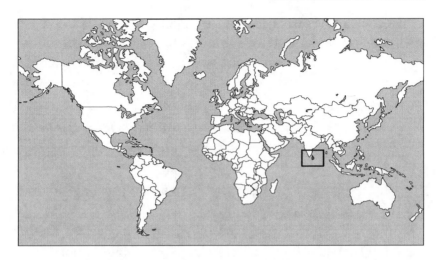

"No to Rape, No to Child Abuse"

The autopsy report later revealed that the child had been raped by a 16-year-old relative and his two friends, and then dumped in the canal, where she drowned.

"It was a ghost town, as if nothing had happened," de Silva told IPS. "I just could not take the silence any longer."

The little girl's body was recovered in the midst of a spell of similar tragedies. Last month [June 2011] six men including a local politician raped a 13-year-old in the southern town of Tangalle, while a 14-year-old girl was repeatedly raped for two consecutive days in another southern town called Akuressa.

De Silva, disturbed by the events and the silence that followed them, took his grievances to the realm of social media, writing on his Facebook wall, "No to rape, no to child abuse."

Soon he had received hundreds of comments and he turned his wall post into a separate page, which has now attracted hundreds of followers who chronicle reports of rape and abuse.

De Silva has also been trying to mobilise media and his colleagues to speak out. "I am doing this as a concerned father and a citizen. I want to inspire and provoke people to shout," he said.

Last month six men including a local politician raped a 13-year-old in the southern town of Tangalle.

Diarietou Gaye, the Senegalese-born country head for the World Bank in Sri Lanka, could not take the silence either.

After numerous conversations with her staff, Gaye took a very unusual step for a representative of an international donor agency—she went public and aired her views on her blog.

"It is about time people start talking about it at work, in the neighbourhood, in school, in religious institutions and in any public or private fora and denounce this degrading act of violence," Gaye told IPS, pointing out that in most cases children were attacked by people known to them, by adults who were supposed to protect them, such as relatives, employers and schoolteachers.

Just three days after her first blog post, police arrested an 80-year-old man who worked as a caretaker at an orphanage in the central town of Mawanella on charges of abusing 15 underage girls. All the victims were below the age of 15 years.

But these are just two instances where ordinary citizens have stepped out of their comfort zones to take on the ugly issue of rape and abuse.

Public Indifference

Despite reports that incidents of rape, especially abuse of minors, are on the rise—police spokesperson Ajith Rohana said that over 700 cases had been reported by mid-2012—many feel that the public has been lukewarm at best, complicit at worst.

"I think Sri Lanka has been conditioned to be immune to violence after 30 years of war," Dilrukshi Handunnetti, a lawyer and writer, told IPS.

It is a view that is shared by the young and old alike, spanning a diversity of race, gender and religion.

"I feel that in Sri Lanka, our collective silence is by no means limited to the issue of rape alone. We, as a people, prefer to be blissfully ignorant and ever resilient, irrespective of the issue. The culture of 'people power' or mass mobilisation clearly missed our shores," Marisa de Silva, a post-graduate student, told IPS.

Handunnetti, who has worked with Transparency International on advocacy issues and regularly takes part in human rights discussions, told IPS she felt that most Sri Lankans seemed programmed to "shut down" when confronted with the topic of sexuality.

"Even at human rights discussions, matters relating to sexuality just fall off the table, no one wants to talk," she said.

Such ignorance—and a refusal to grapple with the truth—can be devastating.

Given the magnitude of the problem, the reaction of the masses has been "woeful".

In Sri Lanka's northern region, which is only just now opening up after three decades of civil war that only ended in May 2009, there is an increase in teenage pregnancies, Saroja Sivachandran, head of the Jaffna-based [Centre for] Women and Development, told IPS.

The organisation has recorded over 400 cases of teen pregnancies and received over 300 reports of rape in the northern region for this year alone. She believes lack of knowledge is the primary reason that leads to abuse.

"These girls and even the boys are naive, they don't know what is out there, but with the war ending, the outside world has crashed into their lives. We have to tell them what is good and what is not," she said.

De Silva admits that a blog or a Facebook page has limited impact in Sri Lanka. "We have to reach out to the regions where these things are happening, we have to somehow get our people to talk and report on this," he stressed.

"But the more we talk, the more people will be aware and perpetrators exposed."

Sporadic protests have been held in Colombo and throughout the suburbs, while a group of activists are planning to write to President Mahinda Rajapaksa, highlighting the issue and seeking a meeting.

But as Sivachandran pointed out, given the magnitude of the problem, the reaction of the masses has been "woeful".

Making a Change

At least in cyber space, the public verdict has been clear—60 percent of participants in web surveys carried out by *Lankadeepa*, a Sinhala newspaper, and the Derana media group, believe that convicted child rapists should be given the death penalty, even though the death sentence is not carried out in the country.

De Silva told IPS that change will take time and will be laboriously slow. "But the more we talk, the more people will be aware and perpetrators exposed."

World Bank's Gaye feels that if a strong-willed leadership is at the mantle of any movement, it will take off, but will succeed only if a majority of the island's citizens take note.

"To make a change, you need strong political will and leadership, which is evident in some parts of Sri Lanka," she said, hastening to add, "if Sri Lanka is serious about becoming the Miracle of Asia, it needs to protect its people and it is the responsibility of each and every Sri Lankan to make sure that this happens."

Young Girls Face Endemic Sexual Violence in Kenya

Katy Migiro

Katy Migiro is a Thomson Reuters journalist based in East Africa. In the following viewpoint, Migiro reports that sexual violence and abuse of young children are widespread in Kenya, where a third of girls and a fifth of boys experience sexual abuse before age eighteen. The problem is exacerbated because much of the public sees violence and domestic abuse within families as normal, according to Migiro. She says that the Kenyan government is trying to set up child protection centers, but that most children and victims do not know where to get help to deal with sexual violence.

As you read, consider the following questions:

1. Where does Migiro get her figures about sexual violence in Kenya?
2. According to Migiro, what percentage of men and women condoned domestic violence?
3. Around the world, what percentage of boys and girls experience sexual violence, according to the United Nations?

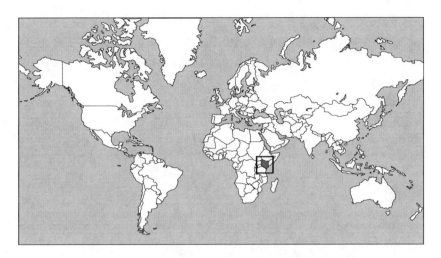

Nearly one in three Kenyan girls experience sexual violence before the age of 18, according to a report launched by the Kenyan government and the United Nations on Wednesday [in November 2012].

Pervasive Violence

Three-quarters of Kenyan children experience physical, sexual or emotional violence, according to the findings of the first nationwide household survey of more than 3,000 young people aged 13 to 24.

"The survey results depict a sobering picture of pervasive and insidious violence that afflicts the entire country," Naomi Shaban, minister of gender, children and social development, said at the launch of the Violence Against Children [in Kenya] survey.

Sexual violence—defined as sexual touching or attempted sex against the child's will or coerced or forced sex—was experienced by 32 percent of Kenyan girls and 18 percent of boys before the age of 18.

This figure is much higher than that of the government's 2008/9 Kenya Demographic and Health Survey which found that one in five women and girls are victims of sexual violence.

Rape is rarely reported in Kenya due to stigma and a lack of faith in the police and the criminal justice system, although the country has strong legislation to protect children from sexual assault.

The survey found that the most common perpetrators were boyfriends or girlfriends, followed by neighbours and family members. One in three girls who were raped became pregnant as a result. Only three percent of sexually abused girls received professional help.

Sexual violence ... was experienced by 32 percent of Kenyan girls and 18 percent of boys before the age of 18.

There was a clear correlation between experience of sexual violence and engagement in risky sexual behaviour. Girls who were victims of unwanted touching or rape were four times as likely as other girls to have multiple sexual partners.

Physical violence—defined as punching, kicking, whipping or being threatened with a weapon—was most widely experienced. Almost six out of 10 children had been physically abused by an authority figure, most commonly teachers.

More than half the respondents had experienced physical violence at the hands of relatives.

Violence Condoned by Society

Most disturbing among the findings was that the majority of children accepted violence in the home as normal, particularly if they themselves had experienced it.

"Much of violence against children ... remains hidden and at times is socially approved or acceptable. That is very sad," said Franklin Esipila, permanent secretary in the ministry of gender, children and social development.

Among girls aged 18 to 24, 49 percent condoned violence by a husband towards his wife. This increased to 56 percent among girls who had experienced childhood violence.

HIV and Sexual Violence in Kenya

Violence against women is not only a public health problem, but also a key vector of the HIV/AIDS pandemic. There is evidence that women and girls in Kenya were at especially high risk of contracting HIV/AIDS during the post-election violence of December 2007 and early 2008. . . .

Some groups of women were more vulnerable to sexual violence and HIV/AIDS transmission than others. Specifically, the situation was extremely serious among the approximately 350,000 displaced people due to the elevated incidence of gang rape. Even after the post-election violence subsided, the risk for women remained high.

In Kenya, as elsewhere, women are socialized to accept, tolerate, and even rationalize domestic violence and to remain silent about such experiences. A recent study finds that 44.1 per cent of national HIV incidence can be attributed to heterosexual sex within existing unions and regular partnerships. These findings confirm a long-hidden reality: that spousal sexual violence, usually initiated by the male partner, is a major source of HIV infection.

A recent study carried out in Kenya reveals that HIV-positive women are subjected to many forms of abuse by their partners. Violence and the threat of violence can hamper women's ability to adequately protect themselves from HIV infection or assert healthy sexual decision making. In addition, women living with HIV are more likely to experience violence due to their HIV status.

Geneva Declaration on Armed Violence and Development,
Global Burden of Armed Violence 2011: Lethal Encounters.
New York: Cambridge University Press, 2011, p. 135.

Unsurprisingly, the figures for boys were even worse. There was 62 percent approval of domestic violence among boys aged 18 to 24 who had not been abused, rising to 65 percent among those who had experienced violence themselves.

"These attitudes must change in order to help mitigate the occurrence of domestic violence, both against women and against children," the report said. "This remains the single greatest area for policy reform at the national level."

"Much of violence against children ... remains hidden and at times is socially approved or acceptable."

Other social attitudes and practices that justify violence against children identified by the survey include the use of violence as a form of discipline, child labour, female genital mutilation, forced marriage, prejudice against disabled children, family breakdown, homophobia and the myth that sex with virgins can cure HIV/AIDS.

Violence Perpetuates Poverty

A 2006 U.N. [United Nations] report found that 14 percent of girls and seven percent of boys around the world experience sexual violence.

"Violence breeds violence," it said. "In later life, child victims of violence are more likely to be victims or perpetrators themselves."

It also found that violence perpetuates poverty, illiteracy and early death.

"The physical, emotional and psychological scars of violence rob children of their chance to fulfil their potential," the report said. "Ending violence will increase opportunities for development and growth."

The Kenyan government said it plans to set up child protection centres, staffed by social welfare officers, across the country to help abused children.

The survey found that just one in four girls and one in eight boys knew where to get help after they were sexually abused.

Childline Kenya, a free national help line for children, receives 40,000 calls a month.

Fighting Child Sexual Abuse in the Caribbean

Tamar Hahn

Tamar Hahn is regional communications officer for Latin America and the Caribbean for UNICEF, the United Nations Children's Fund. In the following viewpoint, she says that there is widespread sexual abuse of children in the Caribbean. Abuse is often covered up, Hahn reports, and people often blame the victim for the abuse. The situation can be exacerbated because mothers who were abused themselves may not feel able to confront the abuse of their children. Hahn says that governments in the region are trying to address the problem and have made some progress.

As you read, consider the following questions:

1. According to Hahn, what do studies in Jamaica and Guyana reveal about attitudes toward sexual violence in those countries?
2. What is the Teddy Bear Campaign?
3. What is Taisha's advice to girls who experience sexual abuse, according to Hahn?

Kingston, Jamaica, 18 May 2012—A nine-year-old boy was systematically raped by his pastor while his mother was at work; an 18-month-old baby boy died of internal damage af-

Tamar Hahn, "Fighting Child Sexual Abuse in the Caribbean," UNICEF, May 18, 2012. Reproduced with permission.

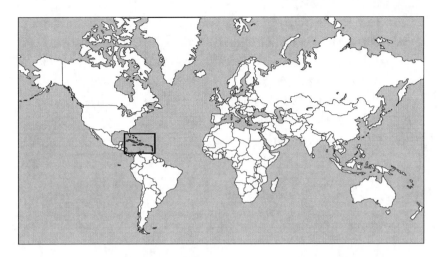

ter being raped by his uncle; a little girl was infected with gonorrhoea, syphilis, herpes and HIV by an uncle who was in and out of prison.

These are some of the cases Sandra Knight, a general practitioner at the paediatric hospital in Kingston, has treated over the years. The abuse tormented her, compelling her to speak out to the press. Dr. Knight's accounts have created an uproar in the Eastern Caribbean, and an avalanche of front-page stories about child sexual abuse has followed.

"I felt that my peers were becoming complacent about this issue," Dr. Knight said. "But I felt I had a tsunami in front of me, which was affecting me because I also have a 6-year-old daughter. I saw these children dying, getting sick, being traumatized for life."

A Silent Emergency

Child sexual abuse is shrouded in secrecy and abetted by shame. While most abuse is hidden and up-to-date statistics are scarce, it is known that nearly 150 million girls and 73 million boys under 18 around the world have experienced forced sexual intercourse or other forms of sexual violence worldwide.

In the Caribbean region, sexual violence against children is greatly underreported, and this abuse is often culturally sanctioned. A study in Jamaica indicated that men often believe they have a right to engage in sex with girls under their care, while children in Guyana reported believing that sexual violence can be blamed on a victim's clothing. Sexual violence against boys is especially underreported, and in some countries, is not even recognized as a crime.

"I saw these children dying, getting sick, being traumatized for life."

"Sexual abuse happens everywhere—at home, school and in other institutions, and has a serious physical, psychological and social impact, not only on girls and boys, but also on the fabric of society. It is one of the main factors that contribute to HIV infections, and that is why it is not surprising that this region has one of the highest prevalence of HIV and AIDS worldwide," said Nadine Perrault, UNICEF Regional Child Protection Adviser for Latin America and the Caribbean. "Our experiences in preventing and responding to sexual abuse have taught us that laws by themselves have been ineffective in protecting children, mainly because of the silence surrounding the issue and the risks that victims face in speaking out—risks such as stigma, shame, harm and further violence. And then, often, children do not know where to turn."

Breaking the Silence

To address the taboo surrounding child sexual abuse, the University of the West Indies in Trinidad and Tobago developed the Teddy Bear Campaign. Using the image of a teddy bear with a Band-Aid over its heart and the tagline 'Break the Silence', this initiative has mobilized a wide range of government and non-governmental partners to protect children from sexual abuse.

Defining Childhood in the Caribbean

We explored the different ways in which childhood might be understood. The majority of the respondents were of the view that children were children at least until the legal age of sexual consent (16 years). However, there was a significant number of people who believe that childhood ends at 13 years. This may help to explain why, in the focus group discussions, some men indicated that they considered girls to be 'legitimate sexual targets' once they reach their teens. Another important issue was that some people believe that childhood ends if a girl becomes pregnant. This suggests that at the conceptual level, for a significant number of people, the state of motherhood is not considered compatible with the status of childhood. This highlights the contradictions and dilemmas that many teenage mothers face as they come to terms with being mothers while they are still children. Juxtaposed against the construction of young motherhood, however, is the reality that these respondents overlooked the fact that for a girl to become pregnant, she must have first been a *child* victim of rape or unlawful sexual intercourse. The study shows that defining child abuse is linked to the way in which childhood is defined.

Adele D. Jones and Ena Trotman Jemmott,
"Child Sexual Abuse in the Eastern Caribbean," UNICEF, 2011, p. 8.

The campaign was discussed during the sub-regional meeting for follow-up to the UN study on violence against children in the Caribbean, which took place in Kingston this week. UNICEF is currently working to expand the reach of this campaign to other countries in the Caribbean.

"Something that has touched me deeply in the discussions that took place during this conference is the really high incidence of sexual abuse in the Caribbean," said Marta Santos Pais, special representative for the secretary-general on violence against children. "I think everyone in the region seems incredibly committed to moving forward and very encouraged by the opportunity to replicate the Teddy Bear Campaign. I am confident that the materials will be replicated and tailored to each country, and we will have greater awareness, greater commitment and fewer cases to be regretted."

Sexual violence against boys is especially underreported, and in some countries is not even recognized as a crime.

Ending a Vicious Cycle

In March 2012, 15-year-old Taisha* was at her sister's house when her 19-year-old brother raped her.

"My mom didn't believe me, and I didn't know what else to do so I decided to go to the police by myself," Taisha said.

Unlike Taisha, most children are brought in by their mothers, many of whom have been victims of abuse themselves. "It is a vicious cycle," said Dr. Knight. "Mothers who have been abused as children, and who did not get help, see this again in their children and don't do anything about it or resent them for it, looking at it in a distorted way. Some of them felt so much shame that they don't want their children to go through that and cover it up."

Taisha is now in a safe home where she is attending school. "If I were to talk to girls in the same situation all around the world, I would tell them to keep their head up high and remember that they are here for a good reason, and they should not let what they've been through stop them in their tracks," she said. "Going to the authorities is the best thing to do because keeping it to yourself will not help."

---

* *Name changed to protect child's identity*

The Supreme Court Is Failing Incest Victims in South Africa

Anna Majavu

Anna Majavu is a writer for SACSIS, a South African nonprofit news agency; she is studying for a master's degree in New Zealand. In the following viewpoint, she reports that the Supreme Court in South Africa reduced the life sentence of a man who raped his stepdaughter on the grounds that the young girl did not resist. Majavu argues that this ruling ignores the nature of incest and the disproportionate power that fathers have over the children in their families. She says the ruling is in line with the way the South African justice system minimizes rape and blames victims.

As you read, consider the following questions:

1. What does Majavu say was the difference between Ndou's final rape of his stepdaughter and earlier rapes?
2. What did the court say was a "compelling and suitable" reason to reduce Ndou's sentence, according to Majavu?
3. On what does Majavu say that politicians blame rape in the townships?

A recent Supreme Court of Appeal judgment has undermined the plight of incest victims who keep quiet about their ordeals after being threatened with death or given tokens by their abusive father figures.

Anna Majavu, "How a Rape Judgement Fails Vulnerable Children All Over South Africa," SACSIS.org.za, November 26, 2012. CC By 2.5 ZA.

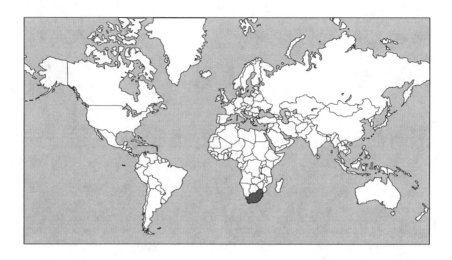

Sentence Reduced

In this recent judgment, Supreme Court of Appeal judge Jeremiah Shongwe—with judges Lex Mpati, Carole Lewis, Belinda van Heerden and Nathan Erasmus concurring—reduced a rapist's life sentence to 15 years. The Limpopo High Court had earlier sentenced Edson Ndou to the mandatory minimum life sentence that is supposed to apply in all cases of rape of a child under the age 18, but Supreme Court of Appeal (SCA) overturned this, accepting Ndou's argument that he "did not use any violence or weapon to force the complainant to submit to having sexual intercourse with him; instead . . . she accepted money and gifts from the appellant".

The judgment is a blow for anti-rape and victim empowerment activist groups. Men occupy the most powerful position in any family. The desire to exercise power and control is often the motivation for committing rape. Incest—whether committed by a father or stepfather—has often remained hidden from police and the courts because of the dominant nature of fathers in families, and because threats by the father rapist are so effective in keeping the victim silent. Despite its hidden nature, incest has remained abhorrent to society and it has always been unthinkable to argue that an incest victim could have consented to being raped.

The judgment detailed how 46-year-old Ndou raped his young stepdaughter in the middle of the night while she was sleeping in a room with her two younger sisters. According to the ruling, it was not the first rape, and he had previously given his stepdaughter sandals, panties and some money after raping her. Ndou had also repeatedly threatened to kill his stepdaughter if she told anyone about the earlier rapes. The only reason that this rape was reported was because his wife caught Ndou committing the crime.

The difference this time was that his wife caught him raping their child and reported him to the police.

Incest . . . has often remained hidden from police and the courts because of the dominant nature of fathers in families.

The Criminal Law Amendment Act is very clear that mandatory minimum life sentences must be imposed except where courts find "compelling and substantial" circumstances, which justify a lesser sentence. The SCA instead relied on dubious, subjective reasons to overturn the life sentence handed down by the lower court.

The judgment states: "she submitted to the sexual intercourse on the occasion in question without any threat of violence. The fact that she had accepted gifts and money from the appellant must have played a role in her submitting to the sexual intercourse. When she was asked whether she had screamed for help, she said that she had not resisted or screamed but simply waited for the appellant to finish what he was doing. She also confirmed that the appellant was drunk and fell asleep next to her after the rape. Thus the degree of the trauma suffered by her cannot be quantified" the judgment stated.

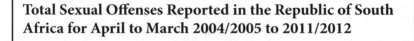

Total Sexual Offenses Reported in the Republic of South Africa for April to March 2004/2005 to 2011/2012

Reported Cases to the South African Police Service (SAPS)

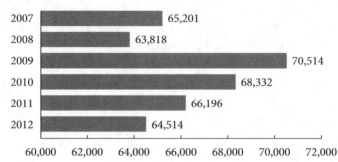

Year	Value
2007	65,201
2008	63,818
2009	70,514
2010	68,332
2011	66,196
2012	64,514

60,000   62,000   64,000   66,000   68,000   70,000   72,000

South African Police Service (SAPS), Crime Statistics Overview RSA 2011–2012. (Online) (Available at http://www.saps.gov.za/statistics/reports/crimestats/2012/downloads/crime_statistics_presentation.pdf) (Accessed on: 26 November 2012)

TAKEN FROM: Linda Daniels, "16 Days of Activism," *Eyewitness News,* November 29, 2012.

Advice Ignored

The judges apparently ignored well-known advice from Rape Crisis and other groups that "abusers seldom need to use force or even threaten force in order to ensure the submission of their child victims". It is not unlikely that a 15-year-old victim, woken violently from her sleep, would be so terrified of the 46-year-old man assaulting her that she would not fight back.

It is also alarming that Judge Shongwe formed his own subjective opinion that the stepfather who raped his daughter, then threatened to kill her before handing over worthless items was a giver of gifts. It is even more peculiar that Shongwe deemed panties not only to be a suitable gift from a rapist, but also a "compelling and substantial" reason to reduce Ndou's sentence.

Because townships remain so underdeveloped, female residents are often sexually assaulted. Reports of rapes mostly don't make the news—rape has become normalised. According to Sokari Ekine, editor of the prominent African blog *Black Looks*, "it is this normalisation of sexual abuse and institutionalized misogyny that allows the police and others in authority to feel comfortable in making statements such as 'she wanted to be raped' and to be wholly negligent in their investigations".

Abusers seldom need to use force or even threaten force in order to ensure the submission of their child victims.

Normalising Rape

When police repeatedly fail to process rape kits or investigate suspects and when judges fail to convict or adequately sentence rapists, this becomes the norm. Politicians normalise rape further by talking vaguely about "the culture of rape" without taking any responsibility for creating safe environments, or when they blame rape on what they describe as the general barbarism or alcoholism of the poor. The law is clear that raping under-18s deserves a life sentence, but there are now judges deciding that if a 15-year-old is given a panty, that is a compelling argument for a lesser sentence.

Unfortunately, there was very little public scrutiny of the SCA decision because the press was preoccupied at that time with interrogating why the Judicial Service Commission had declined to appoint senior counsel Jeremy Gauntlett as a judge. The IFP [a political party in South Africa] even described the Gauntlett issue as "a symptom of an unfolding national tragedy" where lawyers who are "white and bright" are allegedly denied the chance to become judges.

Yet most women and children who are raped are not "white and bright" but part of the poor and working-class black majority whose unsafe living conditions dictate that they will inevitably become victims of sexual violence. The leaders of the three largest political parties—Helen Zille, Mosiuoa Lekota, Jacob Zuma, and Kgalema Motlanthe—show little interest in developing the townships to a livable standard, and are preoccupied with premature electioneering, publicity seeking and quashing internal dissent in their parties. The violence on the streets inevitably spills over into the home.

Politicians normalise rape further by talking vaguely about "the culture of rape" without taking any responsibility for creating safe environments.

These politicians will feature in a multitude of photo opportunities; milking the annual "16 days to end violence against women and children" campaign for as much political capital as possible. But after a few hours in the spotlight, they will return to their secure homes, leaving more women and children to be raped and murdered in the insecure townships.

Still No One to Turn To: Child Sexual Abuse by Aid Workers and UN Peacekeepers

Marlen Suyapa Bodden

Marlen Suyapa Bodden is a human rights attorney and author of the novel The Wedding Gift. *In the following viewpoint, she discusses a 2008 human rights report that found significant levels of sexual abuse of children by United Nations (UN) aid workers. Bodden says that abuse included child prostitution, gang rape, and numerous other abuses. Yet, two years after the report was released, Bodden says, the UN has done little to address the issue and has not even set up a system to receive and investigate complaints. Bodden concludes that the UN needs to move quickly to stomp out sexual violence against children by human rights workers.*

As you read, consider the following questions:

1. What countries did the original Save the Children report investigate?
2. Who did the *Times Online* write about in its coverage of the Save the Children report?
3. What specific steps does Bodden say the United Nations needs to take to address sexual abuse by aid workers?

Aid workers, peacekeepers, and other local and foreign staff associated with the official international community commit significant levels of sexual violence and abuse against children, with much of the abuse going unreported, said Save the Children UK, in a 2008 report (located below [not shown]) based on fieldwork visits to towns, villages, and rural areas in Southern Sudan, the Ivory Coast, and Haiti entitled *No One to Turn To*.

The forms of abuse include rape; sexual slavery, where a child is forced to have sex with an adult by someone else who receives payment; child trafficking linked with commercial sexual exploitation, where a child is transported for the purposes of child prostitution or sexual slavery; child prostitution, where an adult pays money to have sex with a child; "trading sex," where a child is forced to have sex for food and other non-monetary items or services; child pornography, where a child is filmed or photographed performing sexual acts; indecent sexual assault, where an adult touches a child in a sexual manner or makes physical sexual display towards them; and verbal sexual abuse, where an adult says sexually indecent words to a child. According to Save the Children UK, children as young as six are forced to have sex with aid workers and UN peacekeepers in exchange for food, money, and soap.

According to the report, a 15-year-old Haitian girl said to interviewers: "My friends and I were walking by the National Palace one evening when we encountered a couple of humanitarian men. The men called us over and showed us their penises. They offered us 100 Haitian gourdes (US$2.80) and some chocolate if we suck them. I said no, but some of the girls did it and got the money."

When *No One to Turn To* was issued in 2008, there was an outcry in the media and the *Times Online* wrote about a 12-year-old child in the Ivory Coast, "Elizabeth," who was pulled from the road by ten UN peacekeepers and gang-raped.

The report called for the establishment of an international watchdog to investigate the sexual abuse of children by aid workers and peacekeepers. The charity recommended that effective local complaint mechanisms be set up to enable people to report abuses against them and that tackling the root causes of the abuse become a greater priority for governments, donors, and others in the international community.

Children as young as six are forced to have sex with aid workers and UN peacekeepers in exchange for food, money, and soap.

Two years later, however, in the wake of the Haitian and Chilean disasters, little, if anything, has been done to end the sexual abuse of children by aid workers and UN peacekeepers. I contacted Save the Children UK about what it has done to address the problem, but no one bothered to return my call. I also contacted the UN peacekeepers in New York. The response that I received from the UN's Department of Peacekeeping Operations (DPKO), couched in bureaucratic language, sounded as if many meetings have been held, but no action has been taken.

According to DPKO's response, there is a Task Force on Protection from Sexual Exploitation and Abuse. The task force, however, does not specifically focus on child sexual abuse by UN peacekeepers and there is still no mechanism for making complaints and having them investigated. DPKO's response to me stated that a working group of the task force is currently finalizing a guidance document on setting up community-based complaint mechanisms and conducting a review to assess the extent to which organizations and country teams have addressed sexual exploitation and abuse. DPKO did not provide an explanation why two years after *No One to Turn To* was issued a complaint procedure not only is not in place, but is still a work in progress. DPKO's review, further, is not specifically about child sexual abuse by aid workers or UN peace-keepers and no justification has been provided why this review was not conducted and completed in 2008.

Two years later . . . little if anything has been done to end the sexual abuse of children by aid workers and UN peacekeepers.

The UN has a mandate to protect people of all ages who are under its care from violence, sexual violence, and abuse but it is understandable that eradicating those human rights violations is difficult. Preventing sexual violence and abuse of children by UN peacekeepers and aid workers, however, is possible. The UN and aid organizations should take action to implement procedures such as establishing a watchdog to investigate, punish, and remove anyone who commits such acts, and ensuring that each country where UN peacekeepers and aid workers are present has effective and confidential complaint procedures. Until these measures are in place, vulnerable children around the world will continue to be raped, prostituted, trafficked into slavery, and sexually abused by the very people sent to protect and help them.

Periodical and Internet Sources Bibliography

The following articles have been selected to supplement the diverse views presented in this chapter.

Genevieve Carbery	"The Breakup: Why Ireland Is No Longer the Vatican's Loyal Follower," *Time*, July 27, 2011.
Victor Chinyama and Julie Mwabe	"Sexual Violence Affects the Lives of Children at a School in Central Kenya," UNICEF, March 13, 2007. http://www.unicef.org/infobycountry /kenya_39054.html.
Olivia Crellin	"The Caribbean: Shocking Levels of Child Abuse Recognised in Jamaica," Pulsamérica, June 4, 2012. http://www.pulsamerica.co.uk /2012/06/04/the-caribbean-shocking-levels -of-child-abuse-in-jamaica/.
GlobalPost	"Ireland: Pope Calls Sexual Abuse in the Catholic Church 'a Mystery,'" June 17, 2012. http://www.globalpost.com/dispatch/news /regions/europe/ireland/120617/pope-benedict -xvi-irish-catholics-dublin-sexual-abuse-clergy.
Patrick Hruby	"Could the Penn State Abuse Scandal Happen Somewhere Else? Definitely," *Atlantic*, July 16, 2012.
Ernesto Londoño	"Afghanistan Sees Rise in 'Dancing Boys' Exploitation," *Washington Post*, April 4, 2012.
Cam McGrath	"Radical Clerics Seek to Legalise Child Brides," Inter Press Service, November 14, 2012. http://www.ipsnews.net/2012/11/radical -clerics-seek-to-legalise-child-brides/.
Saroj Pathirana	"Sri Lanka's Hidden Scourge of Religious Child Abuse," BBC News, June 1, 2012.
Timothy Williams	"A Tribe's Epidemic of Child Sex Abuse, Minimized for Years," *New York Times*, September 19, 2012.

GLOBALVIEWPOINTS

CHAPTER 3

Sexual Violence and Migration

Sex Trafficking and Forced Prostitution Are Serious Problems in the United Kingdom

Amelia Gentleman

Amelia Gentleman writes on social affairs for the Guardian, *and she was previously the paper's Moscow correspondent. In the following viewpoint, Gentleman reports on a Moldovan woman named Katya who was forced into prostitution and trafficked to the United Kingdom. She was arrested and deported, after which her kidnappers found her, abused her, terrorized her and her family, and re-trafficked her. Gentleman says that the United Kingdom should have granted Katya asylum and suggests that the government is not doing enough to protect trafficking victims.*

As you read, consider the following questions:

1. What is the Poppy Project?
2. While Katya was in detention, what did officials allow her traffickers to do, according to Gentleman?
3. What statistics on trafficking in 2010 does Gentleman cite from the Association of Chief Police Officers?

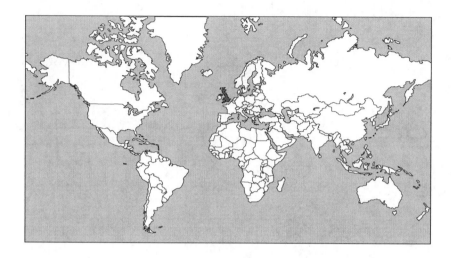

When they assessed her case, British immigration officials knew that Katya, a vulnerable 18-year-old from Moldova, had been trafficked and forced into prostitution, but ruled that she would face no real danger if she was sent back.

UK Government Failures

Days after her removal from the UK [United Kingdom], her traffickers tracked her down to the Moldovan village where she had grown up. She was gang-raped, strung up by a rope from a tree, and forced to dig her own grave. One of her front teeth was pulled out with a pair of pliers. Shortly afterwards she was re-trafficked, first to Israel and later back to the UK.

The Home Office decision last week [in April 2011] to pay her substantial damages has raised serious questions about the way Britain treats trafficked women. The unprecedented case also opens the possibility that other individuals who have been removed from this country and subsequently found themselves exposed to danger in their home country, could attempt to sue the Home Office for damages. The Moldovan woman was first kidnapped by traffickers when she was 14, repeatedly sold on to pimps and other traffickers, and forced to work as a prostitute for seven years in Italy, Turkey, Hungary,

Romania, Israel and the UK. She told the *Guardian* that British police need to do much more to protect women like her and to prevent others from being trafficked into prostitution.

"Just look around you—see how many girls there are like me. They are coming all the time. I see them every day—in tube stations, all made up, early in the morning. Maybe for you it is difficult to see them, but I see them," said Katya (not her real name), in an interview in her solicitor's office. "I think the police should work better to stop this. Why don't you shut down saunas and brothels? Then there would be no prostitutes, no pimps."

The exhaustive account that Katya has given in court documents, explaining how she was targeted, captured and intimidated, reveals the sophisticated methods employed by gangs trafficking vulnerable women from Eastern Europe, Africa and the Far East. It also reveals the danger that these women are often exposed to when the British immigration service opts to remove them.

Kidnapped and Trafficked

Experienced staff at the Poppy Project, which provides specialist support for trafficking victims and which last week learned it was losing its government funding, described her story as among the most disturbing they have encountered. Katya has been diagnosed with post-traumatic stress disorder, but finds therapy sessions too painful to engage with.

> *"Just look around you—see how many girls there are like me."*

She was living with her mother in Moldova when two older men invited her and a friend to a birthday picnic in a nearby forest. Both girls were knocked unconscious, driven to Romania, blindfolded, taken across a river in an inflatable dinghy to somewhere in Hungary, dressed in dark clothes and made to walk through the forest across the border during the night, passing through Slovenia and arriving eventually in Italy.

They were sold on to two separate men. Katya worked first in a flat in Rimini and then on the streets of Milan. After some months, she managed to escape and was sheltered for a while in the Moldovan embassy there, when she discovered she was pregnant.

She chose to return to her family in Moldova to have the child, but her traffickers found her, beat and raped her brother and killed the family dog as punishment for her decision to tell Italian police what happened to her. She discovered that the friend she had been kidnapped with had been murdered by traffickers in Israel who had drugged her and thrown her off a seven-storey building. These experiences terrified her so much that for years she avoided doing anything that might upset her traffickers in case they acted on their threats to hurt her family.

Afraid to Speak

After she gave birth, and sent her daughter to live in relative safety with an aunt, Katya was sent to Turkey to work in a nightclub. She was later smuggled in a lorry to work in a London brothel. During her time working as a prostitute, she was given no money for her work and was not allowed to go anywhere unaccompanied in case she tried to escape. Her clients in London rarely asked about the conditions in which she was working. "The clients, they're drunk, and just come and say, 'Give me this, that'. No one asks: 'How are you?' Some of them asked, 'Why do you do this job?', but I wouldn't answer," she said, explaining that she was afraid that if she appealed to them for help, they might turn out to be friends with the trafficker.

She and the other women—mainly Eastern European, none of them British—never talked of their circumstances among themselves. "I didn't know if the other girls were friends of the trafficker. It was dangerous to speak to the clients or the other girls. There were speakers in the flat where we lived. We didn't talk about anything. Sometimes we were locked up for weeks and weeks, not going out."

[Katya's] traffickers found her, beat and raped her brother and killed the family dog as punishment for her decision to tell Italian police what happened to her.

The brothel, in Harrow, north-west London, was raided a few weeks after she arrived. She was arrested, but she did not reveal the full details of her enslavement to the police because the Kosovar Albanian man who had bought her told her that her family would be in danger if she said anything.

Because officials did not realise Katya had been intimidated by her trafficker, they allowed him to visit her nine times when she was in detention, visits he used to intimidate her further. Although they recognised that she had been trafficked, immigration officials decided to remove her to Moldova, judging that there was no real risk to her safety. A few days after she returned home, her traffickers found her.

"They took me to a forest and I was beaten and raped. Then they made a noose out of rope and told me to dig my own grave as I was going to be killed," Katya's court statement reads. "They tied the noose around my neck and let me hang before cutting the branch off the tree. I really believed I was going to die. They then drove me to a house where many men were staying. They were all very drunk and took turns to rape me. When I tried to resist, one man physically restrained me and pulled my front tooth out using pliers."

The attack ended only when her trafficker told the men they needed to stop as Katya was to be sold in Israel. "I think maybe they did not kill me because I was more valuable alive," her statement reads. Katya, now 26, is thin and pale, but dentists have replaced her tooth, and her other scars are well hidden. "I didn't have too many scars or injuries as the traffickers wanted to keep me looking pretty," she said. After working in Tel Aviv for a while, Katya again escaped before being trafficked to work in a central London flat, where her pimps sold her for £150 an hour; again, she received no money. In 2007 she was detained for a second time by immigration officials, who considered returning her to Moldova, before finally granting her refugee status.

Katya has been interviewed by medical and trafficking experts in preparation for the trial, all of whom found her account credible. Her legal team argued immigration solicitors should have investigated evidence that she was a victim of trafficking and that their decision to return her to Moldova, where she ran the risk of retribution and re-trafficking, was a violation of her rights under article 3 (the right to freedom from torture and inhumane and degrading treatment) and article 4 (the right to freedom from slavery and servitude) of the European Convention on Human Rights. Paul Holmes, the now retired former head of the Metropolitan Police's vice unit, CO14, said in a pre-trial statement that there was already much evidence by 2003 that should have led immigration officials to identify her as a trafficking victim. He said there was "friction" at that time between the immigration service's desire to remove "illegal entrants" to the country, and his department's desire to interview potential victims and get them to testify against traffickers.

Removed and Re-Trafficked

"Our doubt about the effectiveness of prompt removal was exacerbated by the fact that our intelligence-gathering and operational activities had highlighted the fact that in some cases, victims that had been removed were subjected to re-trafficking

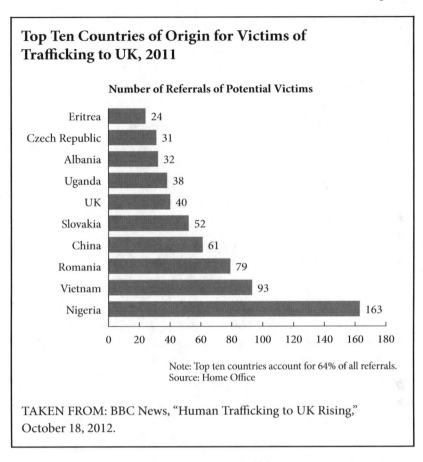

Top Ten Countries of Origin for Victims of Trafficking to UK, 2011

Number of Referrals of Potential Victims

Country	Referrals
Eritrea	24
Czech Republic	31
Albania	32
Uganda	38
UK	40
Slovakia	52
China	61
Romania	79
Vietnam	93
Nigeria	163

Note: Top ten countries account for 64% of all referrals.
Source: Home Office

TAKEN FROM: BBC News, "Human Trafficking to UK Rising," October 18, 2012.

and were being discovered for a second time in London brothels or elsewhere within weeks of their original removal," he said.

Katya's case was due to open last week at the high court in London, but Home Office lawyers agreed to pay substantial, undisclosed damages the day before the scheduled start of the case.

Her solicitor Harriet Wistrich, of legal firm Birnberg Peirce, said she hoped the case would highlight the dangers of unlawful removal and could prompt other claims. Wistrich said she believed the case, which has been two years in preparation, might also educate people about the reality of trafficking of women from Eastern Europe. "People don't believe it's happening on this scale. People don't want to believe it," she said.

21% of the women who came to the [Poppy Project] seeking help had already been sent home and re-trafficked at least once.

There is no clear data to indicate how many trafficked women may be in England and Wales, but research for the Association of Chief Police Officers last year [2010] found clear evidence of 2,600 trafficked victims and of another 9,600 "vulnerable migrants" who might have been trafficked.

The Home Office says there have been improvements in the way immigration officials deal with trafficked women since 2003, and minister Damian Green said: "The UK has become a world leader in fighting trafficking and has a strong international reputation in this field."

But Sally Montier, of the Poppy Project, said the charity was still regularly helping women who were wrongly sent home and re-trafficked. She warned that 21% of the women who came to the charity seeking help had already been sent home and re-trafficked at least once.

"Worryingly, we are seeing an increase in women who have been identified as victims of trafficking but who are in the process of being removed," she said.

Last week's decision to award the Salvation Army the government contract to provide support to trafficked women would lead to the loss of the expertise built up by the Poppy Project over the last eight years, she said. "We are very worried that we will see more women who are not identified as having been trafficked, and who are consequently removed, so that they fall back into the cycle of trafficking and abuse."

Katya's traffickers have not been arrested and she is concerned they could now target her younger sister in Moldova.

She plans to stay in the UK, has signed up for computer courses and English language classes, and is doing voluntary work. Recently she succeeded in bringing her daughter to live with her, but is troubled by the possibility that she could run into the people who forced her into prostitution in London.

She is sceptical about the likelihood that the Home Office decision could force officials to treat trafficking victims with more sensitivity: "If the government cared it would not be closing the Poppy Project. They don't care."

But she adds: "I'm not angry with the government. How can you be angry with the government? I'm angry with my life, the things that have happened."

Sex Trafficking and Forced Prostitution Have Been Overstated as Problems in Europe

Nathalie Rothschild

Nathalie Rothschild is commissioning editor of Spiked. *In the following viewpoint, she argues that trafficking in the European Union is largely a myth. For the most part, she argues, those who work in the sex industry do so voluntarily. Rothschild says that the language of "trafficking" is used as a way to demonize the sex industry, and also as a way to target and criminalize migrants. She concludes that anti-trafficking legislation tends to restrict liberty and harm sex workers and immigrants.*

As you read, consider the following questions:

1. According to Rothschild, what did a major police investigation into trafficking in Ireland discover?
2. According to Nick Mai, why do some migrants choose to work in the sex industry?
3. What evidence does Rothschild provide that sex workers around the globe do not want the trade criminalized?

Nathalie Rothschild, "More Evidence That Trafficking Is a Myth," *Spiked*, April 27, 2009. Reproduced with permission.

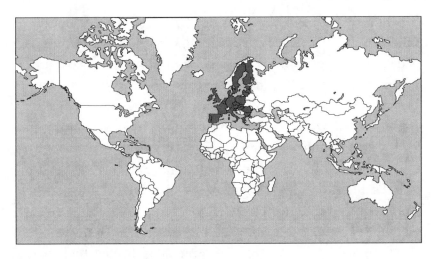

At the beginning of April [2009], just days before the European convention on action against human trafficking came into force in Britain, academics, sex workers and activists from around the world took part in a five-day 'Sex Worker Open University' in east London.

Not Anti-Trafficking—Anti-Migrant

On the first day of film screenings, workshops and discussions on issues related to the sex industry, trafficking was a recurring theme. Participants were keen to debunk the myths of global 'people smuggling' and forced prostitution. The head of the Danish Sex Workers' Interests Organisation claimed that 'very few who work in the sex industry have been trafficked'. Nick Mai, a senior research fellow in migrations and immigrations at London Metropolitan University, asserted that, although anti-trafficking legislation is rolled out in the name of protecting migrants and women, it ultimately amounts to 'anti-migration legislation'. A representative from the [English] Collective of Prostitutes said anti-trafficking campaigners 'use inflated figures and exploit public concern' to push through legislation.

Indeed, even as EU [European Union] member states join forces to combat human trafficking, evidence for its existence is disintegrating. A major police investigation into prostitution in Ireland has failed to find any evidence of organised trafficking there. 'Despite recent claims about large-scale organised trafficking of women and even children to this country', the Irish *Sunday Independent* reported last week, 'the detectives found only two cases where it may have occurred, but they also had doubts after the women involved changed their stories'. Irish police concluded that most of the young foreign women working within the sex industry in Ireland are doing so voluntarily. Perhaps they are motivated by the high pay—prostitutes in Ireland apparently earn between €500 and €600 per day, on average.

Indeed, even as [European Union] member states join forces to combat human trafficking, evidence for its existence is disintegrating.

Embarrasingly, these police findings seem to contest research published just days earlier by Irish anti-trafficking campaigners. They claimed to have identified 102 women and girls as having been trafficked into Ireland for the sex industry over a 21-month period. Many of these women had indeed experienced unacceptable abuse and violence as part of their sometimes dangerous work. But the Irish campaigners used dubious methods to reach the conclusion that the foreign women and girls were 'trafficking victims' and were 'just the tip of the iceberg'. They used a broad UN [United Nations] definition of trafficking, which completely discounts any notion of consent as 'irrelevant' since 'the vast majority of people trafficked for prostitution see little or no viable alternative at the time'.

Presenting Sex Work as Slavery

It is not only in Ireland where claims around organised trafficking and modern-day slavery have turned out to be myths. In the run-up to the 2006 World Cup in Germany, left- and right-wing politicians, Christians and feminists formed an unholy cross-border alliance in an attempt to stop 40,000 'sex slaves' from being forced in to Germany to satiate the lust-filled male football fans. As it turned out, German police uncovered just five cases of 'human trafficking for the purpose of sexual exploitation' during the World Cup—and one of the victims was a German.

At the Sex Worker Open University, Nick Mai pointed out that coercion and exploitation does exist within the sex industry: Some women are indeed forced into it against their will, or certainly have very restricted choices. Yet the emotive term 'trafficking' has become a powerful tool for prostitution abolitionists to win wider public support for their efforts to clamp down on the sex industry as a whole, and to criminalise migrant workers. Anti-trafficking has replaced HIV/AIDS as the abolitionists' trump card.

Mai pointed out that some migrants choose to work in the sex industry in order to avoid exploitation in other industries, where there is frequently low pay and long working hours. Yet migrants tend to become subjects of concern for campaigners only when they enter the sex industry, despite the fact that they can earn significantly more through that line of work than they would as domestic workers or seasonal agricultural workers for instance.

Anti-traffickers appear to believe that sex work in itself is a form of enslavement, and thus presume that foreigners who work in the sex industry in Britain and elsewhere in Europe are doing so against their will. It is telling that one anti-trafficking activist, writing in the *Guardian*, confused a statistic on the number of foreign nationals working in the British sex industry with the number of trafficking victims. She wrote:

113

'Ten to 15 years ago, only 15 per cent of the women in the UK sex trade were trafficked.' Later, a correction to the article said: 'We meant 15 per cent were foreign nationals.'

The same article cited another, already disproved figure: that 80 per cent of women in prostitution in Britain are foreign nationals, most of whom have been trafficked. This estimate was provided by the Poppy Project, set up by the UK Home Office in 2003 to combat trafficking and sexual abuse of women arriving in the UK. The figure is based on a 2002 survey by the Metropolitan Police's Clubs and Vice Unit, which claimed to have discovered that in venues used for prostitution in central London, 70 to 80 per cent of the women were foreign. Similar figures later appeared in a Home Office consultation paper on prostitution.

Anti-traffickers appear to believe that sex work in itself is a form of enslavement.

Both of these studies acknowledged the difficulty of establishing exactly how many women are trafficked into prostitution. And yet, the Poppy Project deduced from its study of women working in the off-street sex industry in one part of London that the trends found there would be reproduced in the same way across the rest of Britain. This is a dubious presumption, to say the least. The Poppy Project and other anti-trafficking warriors tend to presume that foreign women working in the sex industry are, by definition, 'victims of trafficking'; they refuse to see migrants or sex workers as people with agency. In their worldview, there is only room for victims and perpetrators, the abused and abusers.

Forcibly Rescued

Of course, women often enter the sex industry because of a lack of choice; you would be hard-pressed to find young girls who aspire to be prostitutes when they grow up. It would be

Denying Agency

Social helpers consistently deny the agency of large numbers of working-class migrants, in a range of theoretical and practical moves whose object is management and control: the exercise of governmentality. The journeys of women who work in the sex industry are treated as involuntary in a victimising discourse known as 'trafficking', while the experiences of men and transgenders who sell sex are ignored. The work of migrant women in Europe, not only in sex but in housework and caring, is mostly excluded from government regulation and accounts, leaving these workers socially invisible. Migrants working in the informal sector are treated as passive subjects rather than as normal people looking for conventional opportunities, conditions and pleasures, who may prefer to sell sex to their other options. The victim identity imposed on so many in the name of helping them makes helpers themselves disturbingly important figures. Historical research demonstrates how this victimising and the concomitant assumption of importance by middle-class women, which began two centuries ago, was closely linked to their carving out of a new employment sphere for themselves through the naming of a project to rescue and control working-class women.

Laura María Agustín, "Sexual Commotion,"
Sex at the Margins: Migration, Labour Markets
and the Rescue Industry. *New York: Zed Books, 2007, p. 8.*

silly, as many pointed out at the Open University, to romanticise sex work. Yet at the same time, many workers in different industries and sectors, especially poorly paid migrant workers, do not always feel that they have unlimited options available to them. Most people work out of necessity rather than personal choice.

The Irish police investigation suggests, yet again, that theories of mass, organised trafficking are mere speculations. Figures tend to be heavily inflated and are tied to political agendas rather than being grounded in reality. After all, how can a phenomenon for which there is no agreed definition, and which is routinely described as a 'covert activity' that happens in 'the shadow economy', be quantified in any real way? How do you define 'consent' and 'choice' in situations where people set out on journey across the world, unsure about exactly what they will find at the end of it? Why should we expect migrants to avoid hiring so-called 'people smugglers' to take them across borders or to provide them with false documentation when they are denied legal ways of travelling?

Across the globe, serious clampdowns on liberty are occurring in the name of 'combating trafficking'. This became painfully clear at the Open University, where activists from around the world spoke of the challenges posed by anti-trafficking legislation. One woman told of how migrant sex workers in Costa Rica are routinely rounded up and arrested in the name of rooting out trafficking. In Cambodia, anti-trafficking legislation, introduced under pressure from the US Department of State, has led to raids on brothels, with thousands being 'forcibly rescued' by NGOs [non-governmental organisations]. Women at the Empower Foundation, a collective of sex workers in Chiang Mai, Thailand, have reported similar 'rescue missions' by police and charity workers, ending with them being locked up, interrogated and deported without any compensation for them or their dependents.

Anti-traffickers tend to claim that it is only a small minority of privileged, Western sex workers who are against the criminalisation of sex work in general. Yet around the world, thousands of sex workers have organised to campaign for their working rights—from Argentina and Mexico to France and the UK; from Thailand and Cambodia to Malaysia and India. As the organisers of the Sex Worker Open University said: 'The issue of trafficking has been used by some to try to criminalise all sex workers. We contest this simplistic association of all sex work with trafficking and abuse and we support the rights of all migrant workers, whether victims of trafficking or not, and condemn the detention and deportation of those workers.'

It is high time we ended the perverse war on 'trafficking' and started standing up for personal choice and for the right of people to move freely around the world.

Worldwide, Sexual Violence Is Prevalent in Labor Trafficking

Global Freedom Center

The Global Freedom Center is a US organization that works to prevent global trafficking and slave labor. In the following viewpoint, the author says that sexual violence is generally seen only as a component of sex trafficking. However, the viewpoint argues, sexual violence is in fact also often used to intimidate enslaved people in many areas, from domestic workers to farmworkers. The author adds that identifying sexual violence can be an important way to expose situations in which laborers are enslaved or coerced. The viewpoint concludes that professionals need to be trained to ask questions about and identify the use of sexual violence by traffickers.

As you read, consider the following questions:

1. How does the viewpoint define sexual violence?
2. What can traffickers threaten to tell victims' families or communities, according to the viewpoint?
3. How is labor trafficking masked, and what role does the Global Freedom Center say that sexual violence plays in this masking?

Global Freedom Center, *Overlooked: Sexual Violence in Labor Trafficking*, n.d. Reproduced with permission.

Sexual violence is defined as any unwanted sexual act, including but not limited to touching, voyeurism, exhibitionism, sexual assault and rape, perpetrated against a person through force or coercion. Within the workplace generally, sexual violence is used by perpetrators as a mechanism of power and control. Human traffickers use sexual violence, primarily against women and girls but also against men and boys, as both a physical and psychological means to compel labor.

Sexual violence is commonly associated with sex trafficking, where commercial sexual activity comprises the compelled service. Yet with more information on how sexual violence is used as a coercive tool used by labor traffickers, more victims can be identified and offered appropriate services.

Traffickers have used rape as punishment for workers either trying to escape or not completing their production quotas for the day.

How Traffickers Use Sexual Violence to Compel Labor

There are numerous examples of traffickers using sexual violence to compel labor—women in domestic servitude who endure intruders in their room every night, farmworkers in the fields or in employer-owned housing, men and women in manufacturing, women in entertainment clubs, and men at sea for months on fishing vessels. Traffickers use dehumanizing tactics to compel service such as sexual violence and physical force by brutally beating their victims into submission. These assaults essentially serve the same purpose as barbed wire and chains, conveying a trafficker's overt control over the workers and breaking their spirit.

Sexual violence can also be used as a form of psychological coercion to compel labor. Traffickers have used rape as punishment for workers either trying to escape or not completing their production quotas for the day. When rape is used to punish one worker, it also stands to further intimidate other workers and the trafficker never even has to utter a word. This alone is a powerful threat, but compounded by the myriad of other coercive techniques, sexual violence is all the more powerful in compelling work. Additionally, traffickers may threaten to tell victims' family or community about the circumstances of their trafficking, including sexual activity. Sometimes this threat is implied and understood without the traffickers having to communicate it verbally. The fear of rejection by family or community can be so strong that trafficked persons will continue to work, not complain, not try to escape, and become resigned to a life of exploitation or trafficking.

First responders and a wide variety of law enforcement and service providers must be prepared to ask about sexual assault in labor trafficking contexts.

How to Improve Identification

Recognizing sexual violence as a mechanism to compel labor can help to increase identification and the provision of appropriate services. An important first step to improve identification is to broaden awareness of the indicators of labor trafficking generally. Labor trafficking is often easily masked as low-wage work or labor exploitation. Particularly when sexual violence is the silent mechanism compelling labor, trafficking may appear to be low-wage work.

First responders and a wide variety of law enforcement and service providers must be prepared to ask about sexual assault in labor trafficking contexts. Sexual violence is more often addressed by the criminal justice system when it involves an act between strangers or acquaintances but is addressed far less often when it occurs in a workplace setting. Decreased awareness more generally about sexual violence in the workplace extends into the labor trafficking context as well. As a result, professionals in the position to identify and help trafficked persons may not think to ask about sexual violence when presented with labor trafficking cases. Therefore, increased awareness will help professionals to be inclusive of sexual violence in their screenings, questionnaires, interviews, outreach and services.

Conversely, sexual assault service providers have the skills to be able to identify the signs of sexual violence, but may not realize that when it occurs in a workplace setting, it may serve as an identification tool for labor trafficking. Being prepared to ask questions about sexual violence in a labor setting could help to identify someone as trafficked and trigger a range of critical protections and services. An expanded understanding of sexual violence within labor trafficking will allow professionals to extend their services to people who have been labor trafficked.

Sexual assault is such a sensitive issue that it is not readily disclosed even if a professional is poised to screen for it. In the case of trafficked persons, there are even more reasons not to share this information. Traffickers use threats like harm to family members to ensure that trafficked persons never talk about the trafficking or the sexual assault specifically. Traffickers also manipulate their victims, telling them that they will be jailed, deported, or otherwise punished so even once they escape trafficked persons are extremely reluctant to trust others and discuss the circumstances of their trafficking for fear of these consequences. Therefore, using techniques known to build trust with trafficked persons can make disclosure more comfortable and more likely.

To achieve these improvements in identification, anti-trafficking, sexual assault and workers' rights professionals must share their respective expertise with one another and update their screenings, intakes, questionnaires and interviews.

These steps will help identify more trafficked persons and direct them toward comprehensive services and protections that also address the sexual violence they endured.

Sexual Prey in the Saudi Jungle

Walden Bello

Walden Bello is chairman of the Committee on Overseas Workers Affairs of the House of Representatives of the Philippines and a columnist for Foreign Policy in Focus. In the following viewpoint, he reports on the abuse and sexual violence experienced by Filipina maids and domestic workers in Saudi Arabia. Bello says that sexual abuse of domestic workers is common. He argues that the sexual violence is encouraged by the segregation of men and women in Saudi Arabia, by Saudi Arabia's history of slavery, and by the low status of women. Other nations such as India have placed restrictions on domestic workers traveling to Saudi Arabia because of widespread abuse; Bello suggests that the Philippines should do the same.

As you read, consider the following questions:

1. When and how did Saudi Arabia abolish slavery?
2. What is POLO, and how did they fail Lorena, according to Bello?
3. What incident led some Indonesian states to ban recruitment of domestics to Saudi Arabia?

He was an officer in the Saudi Royal Navy assigned to the strategic Saudi base of Jubail in the Persian Gulf, and he wanted to hire a maid. She was a single mom from Mindanao

Walden Bello, "Sexual Prey in the Saudi Jungle," *Foreign Policy in Focus*, February 1, 2011. Reproduced with permission.

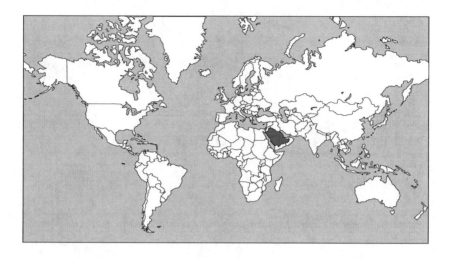

in the Philippines who saw, like so many others, employment in Saudi Arabia as a route out of poverty. When he picked her up at the Dammam international airport last June, little did she know she was entering not a brighter chapter of her life but a chamber of horrors from which she would be liberated only after six long months.

The tale of woe recounted by Lorena (not her real name) was one of several stories of rape and sexual abuse shared by domestic workers with members of a fact-finding team of the Committee on Overseas Workers Affairs of the House of Representatives of the Philippines. The high incidence of rape and sexual abuse visited on the women we met in the shelters run by the Philippine government for runaway or rescued domestic workers in Jeddah, Riyadh, and Al Khobar most likely reflects a broader trend among Filipina domestics. "Rape is common," said Fatimah (also an alias) who had been gang-raped in April 2009 by six Saudi teenagers. "The only difference is we escaped to tell our story while they're still imprisoned in their households."

The working conditions of many domestics, which include 18–22-hour days and violent beatings, cannot but be described except as virtual slavery. Saudi Arabia abolished slavery by royal decree in 1962, but customs are hard to overcome. Royal and aristocratic households continue to treat domestic workers as slaves, and this behavior is reproduced by those lower in the social hierarchy. Apparently among the items of the "job description" of a domestic slave in Saudi is being forced to minister to the sexual needs of the master of the household. This is the relationship that so many young women from the Philippines, Indonesia, India, and other labor-sending Asian countries unwittingly step into when recruitment agencies place them in Saudi homes.

Rape does not, however, take place only in the household. With strict segregation of young Saudi men from young Saudi women, Filipino domestic workers, who usually go about with their faces and heads uncovered, stand a good chance of becoming sexual prey. This is true particularly if they make the mistake of being seen in public alone—though the company of a friend did not prevent the teenagers from snatching Fatimah. And the threat comes not only from marauding Saudi youth but also from foreign migrant workers, single and married, who are deprived by the rigid sexual segregation imposed by the ever-present religious police from normal social intercourse with women during their time in Saudi. Perhaps as a result of the institutionalized repression of Saudi women and their strict subordination to males, Saudi society is suffused with latent sexual violence, much more so than most other societies.

The working conditions of many domestics, which include 18–22-hour days and violent beatings, cannot but be described except as virtual slavery.

Lorena's Tale

Lorena is in her mid-twenties, lithe, and pretty—qualities that marked her as prime sexual prey in the Saudi jungle. And indeed, her ordeal began when they arrived at her employer's residence from the airport. "He forced a kiss on me," she recalled. Fear seized her, and she pushed him away.

He was not deterred. "One week after I arrived," she recounted, "he raped me for the first time. He did it while his wife was away. He did it after he commanded me to massage him and I refused, saying that was not what I was hired for. Then in July he raped me two more times. I just had to bear it because I was so scared to run away. I didn't know anyone."

While waiting for her employer and his wife in a shopping mall one day, Lorena came across some Filipino nurses, whom she begged for help. On hearing her story, they gave her a SIM card and pitched in to buy her phone time.

The employer arrived at that point, but instead of bringing her to the hospital, he said, "You might as well die."

But the domestic torture continued. She would be slapped for speaking Arabic since her employer's wife said she was hired to speak English. She was given just one piece of bread to eat at mealtime and she had to supplement this with scraps from the family's plates. She was loaned to the wife's mother's household to clean the place, and her reward for this was her being raped by the wife's brother; kinship apparently confers the right to rape the servants of relatives. Also during that month, October, she was raped—for the fourth time—by her employer.

She not only had to contend with sexual aggression but with sheer cruelty. Once, while cleaning, she fell and cut herself. With blood gushing from the wound, she pleaded with the employer's wife to bring her to the hospital. The wife refused, and when Lorena asked her to allow her to call her mother in the Philippines, she again said no, telling her this was too expensive. The employer arrived at that point, but instead of bringing her to the hospital, he said, "You might as well die." Lorena had to stanch the wound with her own clothes and treat herself with pills she had brought with her from the Philippines.

Rape During Rescue

Wildly desperate by now, Lorena finally managed to get in touch with personnel of the Philippine Overseas Labor Office (POLO) in Al Khobar. Arrangements were made to rescue her on December 30. That morning, the rescue team from POLO and the local police arrived at the residence. Lorena flagged them frantically from a second-story window and told them she wanted to jump, but the team advised her not to because she could break her leg. That was a costly decision, since the employer raped her again—for the fifth time—even with the police right outside the residence. When she dragged herself to her employer's wife and begged her to keep her husband away from her, she beat her instead, calling her a liar. "I was screaming and screaming, and the police could hear me, but they did not do anything."

When the employer realized that he was about to be arrested, he begged Lorena not to tell the police anything because he would lose his job. He even offered to pay for her ticket home. "I said I would not tell on him and say that he was a good man, just so that he would just let me go," Lorena said. When she was finally rescued moments later, Lorena recounted her ordeal to the POLO team and police, and the employer was arrested.

"These people are influential," she said. "They have a lot of money. I am only a maid."

Released from captivity, Lorena was determined to obtain justice. However, arduous bureaucratic procedures delayed a medical examination to obtain traces of semen right after her rescue. When it was finally conducted, she was given an emer-

Employer and Recruitment Abuses Against Migrant Workers in Bahrain

The plight of many migrant workers in Bahrain begins in their home countries, where poverty and financial obligations entice them to seek higher-paying jobs abroad. Often, they pay local recruitment agencies fees equivalent to approximately 10 to 20 months' wages in Bahrain, even though Bahraini law forbids anyone from charging such fees to workers. It is common for construction and other low-skilled male workers to pay such fees, although uncommon for domestic workers, who tend to come to Bahrain through formal recruitment agencies. The debt that many workers incur to pay recruitment agencies and airfare means they feel compelled to stay in jobs despite unpaid wages or unsafe housing and worksite conditions for months and even years.

Once in Bahrain, migrants depend on regular payment of their salaries to meet their own immediate financial needs and those of their families at home, or to meet monthly loan repayments. Workers indicated that the problem of unpaid wages tops the list of their grievances. Although nonpayment of wages is a criminal as well as civil offence in Bahrain, some employers withhold wages from migrant workers for many months. Without an income source, migrant workers take on more debt to cover basic needs. . . . Out of 62 migrant workers whom Human Rights Watch interviewed, 32 reported that their employers withheld their wages for between three to ten months.

Human Rights Watch, "For a Better Life: Migrant Worker Abuse in Bahrain and the Government Reform Agenda," October 1, 2012.

gency contraceptive pill—an indication, said the POLO officer who led the rescue, that seminal traces had been found in and on her. Also, the examination revealed contusions all over her body and bite marks on her lips.

The criminal investigation is still ongoing and the employer, who has been identified as Lt. Commander Majid Al-Juma-in, is still in jail at the Dammam police station. Lorena is worried that the evidence might be tampered with. "These people are influential," she said. "They have a lot of money. I am only a maid. They said they could put me in prison." Her fear is palpable. Her greatest wish is to be repatriated, but she knows she must stay till he is convicted and sentenced to death.

For the many who have already been raped and degraded sexually, however, a move to prevent the deployment of more women to Saudi Arabia comes too late.

Decision Point

Other governments have begun to take drastic steps to protect their citizens in Saudi Arabia. Owing to numerous cases of abuses of its nationals, India has banned the deployment of women under 40 to Saudi Arabia. After a much-publicized case in which an Indonesia domestic worker suffered internal bleeding and broken bones from a ferocious beating by her employer, who pressed a hot iron on her head and slashed her with scissors, two labor-exporting Indonesian states, West Nusa Tenggara and West Java, banned the recruitment of domestics for employment in Saudi Arabia last December. Earlier, in October, the Sri Lankan ministry of labor backtracked from an agreement arrived at between the Saudi national recruitment agency and the Sri Lankan labor federation, asserting that the terms of the agreement were unfavorable to the Sri Lankan domestics and the Sri Lankan economy. This led the Saudis to indefinitely freeze recruitment from Sri Lanka.

These moves by other governments have led to greater demand for Filipino domestic workers. While the informal policy of the Philippine government has been to slow down the recruitment of domestics to Saudi Arabia, legal and illegal recruiters, many of them tied to Saudi interests, have been trying to step it up. The new Aquino administration may soon reach a critical decision point on the issue of Saudi recruitment since the amended act on overseas workers requires the Department of Foreign Affairs to certify that a country is taking steps to protect labor rights if workers are to be deployed there. With its hideous record and its resistance to expanding coverage of its labor code to domestic workers, Saudi Arabia will not likely be certified.

For the many who have already been raped and degraded sexually, however, a move to prevent the deployment of more women to Saudi Arabia comes too late. Lorena may well secure the conviction of Lt. Commander Majid, but that will not restore her to her former self. As Fatimah put it in a handwritten note she passed on to the team, although her tormentors had been sentenced to seven years' imprisonment and 2500 lashes each, "there's no equivalent amount for what they've done. They destroyed my life, my future."

Thailand: Addressing Sexual Violence in Mae La Refugee Camp

IRIN

IRIN, the Integrated Regional Information Networks, is a humanitarian news and analysis service of the United Nations. In the following viewpoint, IRIN reports on sexual violence in Burmese refugee camps on the Thai border. IRIN says that a sexual and gender-based violence committee (SGBV) was established in the camp to handle reports of rape and domestic violence. The SGBV has made progress in reducing sexual violence and is also providing education for men and women on women's rights.

As you read, consider the following questions:

1. According to IRIN, what aggravates sexual violence and domestic abuse at Mae La?
2. What happens with serious criminal cases brought to the SGBV?
3. What does the SGBV lack sufficient funds to do, according to Myint Aye?

Mae La, 15 January 2009 (IRIN)—Mae La camp, the largest of nine for Burmese refugees on the Thai border, resembles a small thatched city, now more than a decade old,

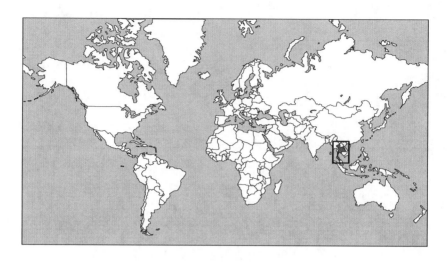

with a population of 50,000 registered and non-registered residents, according to camp officials and the UN Refugee Agency (UNHCR).

Mae La suffers from a significant degree of sexual violence and domestic abuse, aggravated by frustration born of the inability to return to Myanmar, live and work openly in Thai society, or resettle in other countries, according to aid workers.

A Sexual and Gender Based Violence Committee (SGBV) was established in the camp in 2003 with support from UNHCR.

"For a long time, we had been informally helping people in the camp who had been abused," Myint Aye, committee chairwoman, told IRIN. Now it has 15 members, five of them men, and two interns.

While most of the camp residents identify themselves as ethnic Karen, many are Christian, Catholic, Muslim and Buddhist, said Soe Win, a Muslim member of SGBV. "I wanted to work with the committee as I was witnessing so much violence and abuse in the Muslim community and wanted to help," he said.

"We started the committee because we saw there were so many underage rapes and so much domestic violence in the camp," Myint Aye said.

The SGBV said it was getting numerous cases, although fewer than before the programme in 2003, but many more went unreported. "The committee acts as a first responder to acts of abuse," said Alexander Novikau, associate protection officer in the UNHCR Mae Sot office.

"In most cases, abused people, principally women and children, now come to us for assistance," Myint Aye said. "If it's a domestic violence case, we contact the section leader in the camp and the camp security office. . . . If the victim is scared [or] she will be further assaulted, we turn to the Karen women's organisation, which provides a safe house."

"We started the committee because we saw there were so many underage rapes and so much domestic violence in the camp."

Serious criminal cases, mostly involving rape, are referred to the International Rescue Committee Legal Assistance Centre—a project within the camp and supported by UNHCR—which provides legal assistance and advice. If there are injuries, Aide Médicale Internationale (AMI), which maintains two medical facilities in the camp, including a mental health project, provides assistance and refers sufferers to hospitals in Mae Sot if evidence needs to be taken or the injuries are serious.

"If the crime is extremely serious," said Myint Aye, "the perpetrator could enter the Thai justice system either in a court at Mae Sot or another nearby city."

"In some cases, we also engage in mediation and help in the process of reconciliation between the victim and the perpetrator," said Juna, vice chairwoman of SGBV.

Rights Training

The SGBV is not only involved in supporting the abused. "We've received many kinds of training ourselves, in women's and children's rights by the UN and the Legal Assistance Centre," said Myint Aye. "In turn, we now provide training to women in the camp so they know their rights," she said. "We also provide the same training to men so they know about a woman's rights."

SGBV also played a prominent role during the 16-day campaign to eliminate violence against women, from 25 November to 10 December 2008. "Through songs and debates, we joined other groups in raising general awareness about women's rights and the importance of stamping out domestic violence and sexual abuse," said Myint Aye.

"We now provide training to women in the camp so they know their rights."

While the group receives general funding from UNHCR, it is eager to increase public awareness by producing educational posters and increasing outreach. "We also lack sufficient funds to help rape victims or those seriously injured who are sent to Mae Sot hospital [60km away] for tests or treatment and are often without sufficient clothing. Currently we can't do these things because we don't have the money."

Nevertheless, the SGBV committee takes pride in its accomplishments. "If we didn't have the funding we are getting now we would feel like helpless orphans."

Periodical and Internet Sources Bibliography

The following articles have been selected to supplement the diverse views presented in this chapter.

AsiaNews.it	"Saudi Arabia, 70% of Filipino Domestic Workers Suffer Physical and Psychological Violence," March 17, 2012. http://www.asianews.it/news-en/Saudi-Arabia,-70-of-Filipino-domestic-workers-suffer-physical-and-psychological-violence-24260.html.
Gethin Chamberlain	"Sri Lankan Guards 'Sexually Abused Girls' in Tamil Refugee Camp," *Guardian*, December 19, 2009.
Isabel Debre	"For Women, Refuge Often Includes Rape," care2, February 19, 2013. http://www.care2.com/causes/for-women-refuge-often-includes-rape.html.
Human Rights Watch	"Saudi Arabia: Domestic Worker Brutalized," September 2, 2010. http://www.hrw.org/news/2010/09/02/saudi-arabia-domestic-worker-brutalized.
Human Rights Watch	"US: Sexual Violence, Harassment of Immigrant Farmworkers," May 16, 2012. http://www.hrw.org/news/2012/05/15/us-sexual-violence-harassment-immigrant-farmworkers.
Brooke Magnanti	"I Worked in the Sex Trade, Does That Make Me 'Trafficked'?," *Telegraph*, October 18, 2012.
Richard Spencer	"Fear of Rape 'Driving Syria Refugee Crisis,'" *Telegraph*, January 14, 2013.
Amelia Thomson-DeVeaux	"Hundreds of Women and Girls Raped in Haitian Refugee Camps," care2, January 6, 2011. http://www.care2.com/causes/hundreds-of-women-and-girls-raped-in-haitian-refugee-camps.html.

CHAPTER 4

Sexual Violence and Political Violence

Resolution 1820

United Nations Security Council

The United Nations (UN) Security Council is the UN body charged with maintaining peace and security. In the following viewpoint, the Security Council states its opposition to the use of sexual violence in armed conflicts and lists some of the ways it hopes to reduce and prevent such violence. The viewpoint states that sexual violence as a tactic of armed conflict is a war crime and that the UN should document instances of sexual violence and work to eliminate such violence against women and children especially.

As you read, consider the following questions:

1. According to the viewpoint, for what reasons are women and girls targeted for sexual violence in armed conflicts?
2. To what does the policy of zero tolerance mentioned in this viewpoint apply?
3. What important role does the viewpoint say that the Peacebuilding Commission can play in addressing sexual violence in wartime?

*T*he Security Council, . . .

Guided by the purposes and principles of the Charter of the United Nations,

Based on UN document "Resolution 1820," United Nations Security Council, 2008. Cengage Learning is responsible for the adaptation.

Reaffirming also the resolve expressed in the 2005 World Summit outcome document to eliminate all forms of violence against women and girls, including by ending impunity and by ensuring the protection of civilians, in particular women and girls, during and after armed conflicts, in accordance with the obligations States have undertaken under international humanitarian law and international human rights law;

Recalling the commitments of the Beijing Declaration and Platform for Action (A/52/231) as well as those contained in the outcome document of the twenty-third special session of the United Nations General Assembly entitled "Women 2000: Gender Equality, Development and Peace for the Twenty-first Century" (A/S-23/10/Rev.1), in particular those concerning sexual violence and women in situations of armed conflict;

Reaffirming also the obligations of States Parties to the Convention on the Elimination of All Forms of Discrimination Against Women, the Optional Protocol thereto, the Convention on the Rights of the Child and the Optional Protocols thereto, and *urging* states that have not yet done so to consider ratifying or acceding to them,

Noting that civilians account for the vast majority of those adversely affected by armed conflict; that women and girls are particularly targeted by the use of sexual violence, including as a tactic of war to humiliate, dominate, instil fear in, disperse and/or forcibly relocate civilian members of a community or ethnic group; and that sexual violence perpetrated in this manner may in some instances persist after the cessation of hostilities;

Recalling its condemnation in the strongest terms of all sexual and other forms of violence committed against civilians in armed conflict, in particular women and children;

Reiterating deep concern that, despite its repeated condemnation of violence against women and children in situations of armed conflict, including sexual violence in situations of armed conflict, and despite its calls addressed to all parties to armed conflict for the cessation of such acts with immedi-ate effect, such acts continue to occur, and in some situations have become systematic and widespread, reaching appalling levels of brutality,

Recalling the inclusion of a range of sexual violence of-fences in the Rome Statute of the International Criminal Court and the statutes of the ad hoc international criminal tribunals,

---

Women and girls are particularly targeted by the use of sexual violence, including as a tactic of war.

Reaffirming the important role of women in the preven-tion and resolution of conflicts and in peacebuilding, and *stressing* the importance of their equal participation and full involvement in all efforts for the maintenance and promotion of peace and security, and the need to increase their role in decision making with regard to conflict prevention and reso-lution,

Deeply concerned also about the persistent obstacles and challenges to women's participation and full involvement in the prevention and resolution of conflicts as a result of vio-lence, intimidation and discrimination, which erode women's capacity and legitimacy to participate in post-conflict public life, and acknowledging the negative impact this has on du-rable peace, security and reconciliation, including post-conflict peacebuilding,

Recognizing that States bear primary responsibility to re-spect and ensure the human rights of their citizens, as well as all individuals within their territory as provided for by rel-evant international law,

Reaffirming that parties to armed conflict bear the primary responsibility to take all feasible steps to ensure the protection of affected civilians,

Welcoming the ongoing coordination of efforts within the United Nations system, marked by the inter-agency initiative

Sexual Violence as a Tactic of War

Few other strategies can so fundamentally unravel the fabric of society [as sexual violence]. This is because sexual violence encapsulates the violation of multiple taboos, including but not limited to those involving rape. Other forms of sexual violence encompass exploitation and abuse through sexual slavery, forced pregnancy, forced marriage, mutilation, cannibalism, violation of breast-feeding or pregnant and elderly women, the forcing of children to commit rape of others, or family members to commit incest. In armed conflict, rape is often part of a systematic campaign of terror, resulting in mass or collective rape. Gang rape is especially horrific. It involves multiple perpetrators sexually assaulting a particular victim and results in devastating physical and psychological consequences. Sexual assaults also leave victims at risk of HIV/AIDS . . . and sexually transmitted diseases. Dealing with the health and psychosocial consequences of sexual violence is an urgent need, but most countries lack the specialized surgical resources.

Janie L. Leatherman, Sexual Violence and Armed Conflict.
Malden, MA: Polity Press, 2011, p. 8.

"United Nations Action against Sexual Violence in Conflict," to create awareness about sexual violence in armed conflicts and post-conflict situations and, ultimately, to put an end to it,

1. *Stresses* that sexual violence, when used or commissioned as a tactic of war in order to deliberately target civilians or as a part of a widespread or systematic attack against civilian populations, can significantly exacerbate situations of armed conflict and may impede the restoration of international peace and security, *affirms* in this regard that effective

steps to prevent and respond to such acts of sexual violence can significantly contribute to the maintenance of international peace and security, and *expresses its readiness*, when considering situations on the agenda of the council, to, where necessary, adopt appropriate steps to address widespread or systematic sexual violence;

2. *Demands* the immediate and complete cessation by all parties to armed conflict of all acts of sexual violence against civilians with immediate effect;

3. *Demands* that all parties to armed conflict immediately take appropriate measures to protect civilians, including women and girls, from all forms of sexual violence, which could include, inter alia, enforcing appropriate military disciplinary measures and upholding the principle of command responsibility, training troops on the categorical prohibition of all forms of sexual violence against civilians, debunking myths that fuel sexual violence, vetting armed and security forces to take into account past actions of rape and other forms of sexual violence, and evacuation of women and children under imminent threat of sexual violence to safety; and *requests* the secretary-general, where appropriate, to encourage dialogue to address this issue in the context of broader discussions of conflict resolution between appropriate UN officials and the parties to the conflict, taking into account, inter alia, the views expressed by women of affected local communities;

Sexual violence . . . can significantly exacerbate situations of armed conflict.

---

4. *Notes* that rape and other forms of sexual violence can constitute a war crime, a crime against humanity, or a constitutive act with respect to genocide, *stresses the need for* the exclusion of sexual violence crimes from amnesty provisions in the context of conflict resolution processes, and *calls upon* Member States to comply with their obligations for prosecut-

ing persons responsible for such acts, to ensure that all victims of sexual violence, particularly women and girls, have equal protection under the law and equal access to justice, and *stresses* the importance of ending impunity for such acts as part of a comprehensive approach to seeking sustainable peace, justice, truth, and national reconciliation;

5. *Affirms its intention*, when establishing and renewing state-specific sanctions regimes, to take into consideration the appropriateness of targeted and graduated measures against parties to situations of armed conflict who commit rape and other forms of sexual violence against women and girls in situations of armed conflict;

Rape and other forms of sexual violence can constitute a war crime.

---

6. *Requests* the secretary-general, in consultation with the Security Council, the Special Committee on Peacekeeping Operations and its working group and relevant States, as appropriate, to develop and implement appropriate training programs for all peacekeeping and humanitarian personnel deployed by the United Nations in the context of missions as mandated by the council to help them better prevent, recognize and respond to sexual violence and other forms of violence against civilians;

7. *Requests* the secretary-general to continue and strengthen efforts to implement the policy of zero tolerance of sexual exploitation and abuse in United Nations peacekeeping operations; and *urges* troop- and police-contributing countries to take appropriate preventative action, including pre-deployment and in-theater awareness training, and other action to ensure full accountability in cases of such conduct involving their personnel;

8. *Encourages* troop- and police-contributing countries, in consultation with the secretary-general, to consider steps they

could take to heighten awareness and the responsiveness of their personnel participating in UN peacekeeping operations to protect civilians, including women and children, and prevent sexual violence against women and girls in conflict and post-conflict situations, including wherever possible the deployment of a higher percentage of women peacekeepers or police;

9. *Requests* the secretary-general to develop effective guidelines and strategies to enhance the ability of relevant UN peacekeeping operations, consistent with their mandates, to protect civilians, including women and girls, from all forms of sexual violence and to systematically include in his written reports to the council on conflict situations his observations concerning the protection of women and girls and recommendations in this regard;

10. *Requests* the secretary-general and relevant United Nations agencies, inter alia, through consultation with women and women-led organizations as appropriate, to develop effective mechanisms for providing protection from violence, including in particular sexual violence, to women and girls in and around UN-managed refugee and internally displaced persons camps, as well as in all disarmament, demobilization, and reintegration processes, and in justice and security sector reform efforts assisted by the United Nations;

11. *Stresses* the important role the Peacebuilding Commission can play by including in its advice and recommendations for post-conflict peacebuilding strategies, where appropriate, ways to address sexual violence committed during and in the aftermath of armed conflict, and in ensuring consultation and effective representation of women's civil society in its country-specific configurations, as part of its wider approach to gender issues;

12. *Urges* the secretary-general and his special envoys to invite women to participate in discussions pertinent to the prevention and resolution of conflict, the maintenance of

peace and security, and post-conflict peacebuilding, and encourages all parties to such talks to facilitate the equal and full participation of women at decision-making levels;

13. *Urges* all parties concerned, including Member States, United Nations entities and financial institutions, to support the development and strengthening of the capacities of national institutions, in particular of judicial and health systems, and of local civil society networks in order to provide sustainable assistance to victims of sexual violence in armed conflict and post-conflict situations;

Parties to armed conflicts [should] implement their responsibilities . . . by immediately and completely ceasing all acts of sexual violence.

---

14. *Urges* appropriate regional and sub-regional bodies in particular to consider developing and implementing policies, activities, and advocacy for the benefit of women and girls affected by sexual violence in armed conflict;

15. *Also requests* the secretary-general to submit a report to the council by 30 June 2009 on the implementation of this resolution in the context of situations which are on the agenda of the council, utilizing information from available United Nations sources, including country teams, peacekeeping operations, and other United Nations personnel, which would include, inter alia, information on situations of armed conflict in which sexual violence has been widely or systematically employed against civilians; analysis of the prevalence and trends of sexual violence in situations of armed conflict; proposals for strategies to minimize the susceptibility of women and girls to such violence; benchmarks for measuring progress in preventing and addressing sexual violence; appropriate input from United Nations implementing partners in the field; information on plans for facilitating the collection of timely, objective, accurate, and reliable information on the use of

sexual violence in situations of armed conflict, including through improved coordination of UN activities on the ground and at headquarters; and information on actions taken by parties to armed conflict to implement their responsibilities as described in this resolution, in particular by immediately and completely ceasing all acts of sexual violence and in taking appropriate measures to protect women and girls from all forms of sexual violence;

16. *Decides* to remain actively seized of the matter.

German Women Raped by Soviet Soldiers During World War II Still Struggle with Trauma

Siobhán Dowling

Siobhán Dowling is a German-based editor and journalist who has written for the Guardian, Spiegel, *GlobalPost, and many other publications. In the following viewpoint, she discusses the widespread rape of German women by soldiers of the Soviet army during World War II. A new German film is bringing attention to the issue, and researchers are making new efforts to find elderly victims and learn their stories. Dowling says that there is some resistance to seeing Germans as victims during World War II. She also says that wartime rapes can be extremely traumatic, and that many women continue to suffer trauma for years or decades after the attacks.*

As you read, consider the following questions:

1. What is *Anonymous*, as discussed in this viewpoint?
2. Who is Monika Hauser?
3. Who committed rapes of German women in western Germany, according to Dowling?

Siobhán Dowling, "Sexual Violence in World War II: New German Study Looks at Rape Trauma 60 Years On," *Spiegel*, October 22, 2008. Reproduced with permission.

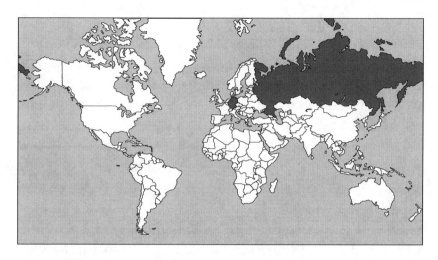

Germany in the spring of 1945. [Adolf] Hitler's Nazi regime was on the brink of defeat in the catastrophic war it had launched six years earlier. After invading and occupying large swathes of Eastern Europe and the Soviet Union—and murdering tens of millions of people in the process—the German army was retreating, and the Red Army [referring to the Soviet army] was following hot on its heels, intent on revenge.

A Woman in Berlin

Sweeping across German territory, many of the Russian soldiers burned, killed, looted. And they also raped German women. The Soviets, of course, weren't the only ones; soldiers from other Allied armies were also guilty of sexual violence as they moved into Germany from the west. But most agree that the problem was particularly acute in eastern Germany. Historians estimate that close to 2 million German women and girls were raped in the closing months of the war, many repeatedly.

This week [in October 2008] a new film, called *A Woman in Berlin*, opens in Germany which deals with the story of one of those women. The film is based on *Anonymous*, an autobiographical account, originally published by a German journalist and editor in the 1950s, describing her experiences between April and June 1945. When it was originally published, reaction was overwhelmingly negative, prompting the author to forbid it from being republished during her lifetime. She died in 2001 and the book hit the shelves again in 2003, going on to become a best seller.

The woman, played by Nina Hoss in the film (the film's North American release date is still pending though it was shown at the Toronto International Film Festival in September), is raped several times by Red Army soldiers before forming a liaison with a Russian officer in order to protect herself from further attacks. While the film tries to turn this into a love story of sorts, in the book the relationship is purely functional.

Historians estimate that close to 2 million German women and girls were raped in the closing months of the war, many repeatedly.

"Their Stories Will Be Heard"

Whether or not the film is strictly accurate, it seems certain to open up the theme of World War II rapes to a much wider audience. And that is exactly what Dr. Philipp Kuwert is hoping for. He is the director of a new research project, based at the University of Greifswald in eastern Germany, which is studying the trauma of women raped during that period. The study has been in the planning stages for over two years and Kuwert decided to launch it officially on Monday to coincide with the release of the film. "It's important to reach the women," he told *Spiegel Online*.

With the events in question dating back 63 years, Kuwert knows that only a small minority of the women who were the victims of sexual violence in those months can be found. Encouragingly, however, since Monday his team has already been contacted by a number of elderly women who want to participate in the project.

The interviews with the women will be carried out by two female PhD students and will be strictly confidential. Kuwert is seeking to find out exactly what these women experienced, how the rapes affected the victims' quality of life and the extent of their trauma. While the study is not designed to provide direct therapy, he is convinced that merely talking about their experiences can still be of benefit to the victims of sexual violence even decades later.

"Their stories will be heard," he says. "This produces a kind of healing effect, known as social acknowledgement of trauma."

"Their stories will be heard," he says. "This produces a kind of healing effect, known as social acknowledgement of trauma."

The project has been given added impetus by the backing of Dr. Monika Hauser, whose group Medica Mondiale helps traumatized women and girls who have experienced sexual violence in conflict zones. Hauser, who recently won the Alternative Nobel Prize—an international award given to those helping people in other disciplines than those recognized by the official Nobel Prize—contacted Kuwert, he says, expressing hope that the project could help to break the taboo associated with the World War II rapes.

"Not Just from a German Point of View"

Kuwert admits that the topic of German victims of the murderous war perpetrated by Nazi Germany is a sensitive and at times ambivalent one in the light of the terrible suffering of "the primary victims," particular the six million Jews mur-

Rape in Germany and Vietnam

Complicating recognition and prosecution of war rape is the obvious fact that not all militaries that commit this crime will find themselves subject to an international war crimes tribunal; additionally, when the "losers" of a war have been the victims of such crimes, these rape victims do not garner the same recognition as more sympathetic victims. A case in point is German women who were raped after World War II, primarily by occupying Soviet forces. Though numerous rapes (some historians describing them as being of "massive incidence") of German women occurred, they have not received much attention from international audiences. Hesitation to recognize crimes against German women is surely due to the legitimate suspicion of historians of the German past toward "any narrative that might support postwar Germans' self-perception as victims insofar as it might participate in a dangerous revival of German nationalism, whitewash the Nazi past, and normalize a genocidal war," [in the words of Atina Grossmann]. . . .

Not unrelated are the war rapes committed by militaries that never find themselves forced to submit to the jurisdiction of international tribunals. This is the circumstance that describes the widespread rapes by American GIs [service members] against Vietnamese civilians and POWs [prisoners of war] that occurred during the Vietnam War. However, not only did international juridical discourse overlook these crimes against Vietnamese women by U.S. forces directly after the time of the war, but recent feminists and other activists working against war rape as well as historians have continued to ignore this well-documented crime.

Gina Marie Weaver,
Ideologies of Forgetting: Rape in the Vietnam War.
Albany, NY: State University of New York Press, 2010, p. 5.

dered in the Holocaust. "It's very difficult for Germans to classify themselves as some kind of victim of the war."

There are many accounts of the SS and German soldiers raping women during the war and Kuwert emphasizes that he does not want to paint Germans as the only victims of sexual violence. The nationality of the victim and the perpetrator is not the focus. "It's not important for the scientific study if it was a Russian soldier in Germany or a German soldier in Eastern Europe," he says. "We have contact with projects in Eastern Europe, in the Ukrainian town of Donetsk, and in St. Petersburg. So it's not just from a German point of view."

While the film *A Woman in Berlin* deals with the Red Army rapes in the East, Kuwert points out that women in western Germany were also the victims of sexual violence. There were hundreds of trials of French and US soldiers for rapes committed in the first months of 1945, though the British armed forces had fewer such cases. While there was also some punishment of Russian soldiers, including executions, most got away with their crimes.

In East Germany, these rapes were particularly taboo because the Red Army was officially regarded as an army of liberation, freeing the Germans from the scourge of fascism and creating a Communist state. "In East Germany, women did not have any official acknowledgement, whereas in the West it was more possible to talk about it," Kuwert says. However, he points out that "sexual violence is always stigmatized," and the rapes were rarely talked about in any part of Germany.

The experience of rape during conflict is often particularly traumatic because the women have no access to any therapy.

In the book *Anonymous*, the narrator, describes how the German women initially talked freely about their experiences with each other. Then the men came home from the front and the rapes became a source of shame—a family secret. Kuwert acknowledges that there can be a difference between wartime rape and other rapes because women feel freer to discuss it.

However, he points out that the experience of rape during conflict is often particularly traumatic because the women have no access to any therapy—and because they are afraid they will also be killed. Kuwert's previous research shows that around half of women raped during war develop post-traumatic stress disorder. "That is very high, compared to say 10 percent of those involved in a serious car crash. Only torture is more severe."

This post-traumatic stress can manifest itself in nightmares or flashbacks, where the woman feels she is once again experiencing the attack. "She can smell the alcohol on the breath of the rapist and it doesn't feel as if it is happening 60 years ago, but now," he says.

The victims can develop a number of health problems, including depression and anxiety. Kuwert is also interested in why some women are particularly resilient after these experiences and do not suffer the same trauma. "We will look at whether they have forgiven their persecutors."

Colombia Has Failed to Address Sexual Violence Committed During Its Battle Against Insurgents

Amnesty International

Amnesty International is an international human rights organization. In the following viewpoint, the author reports that Colombia has not made progress in bringing to justice those who committed acts of sexual violence during the country's war against insurgents. Amnesty International says that Colombia has laws in place to prosecute perpetrators but has been unwilling to implement them. Amnesty International worries that the move to make the military responsible for some aspects of investigating sexual crimes committed during the war will further hamper investigations.

As you read, consider the following questions:

1. According to the author, why are women targets of sexual violence in the context of Colombia's armed conflict?

2. Why don't women in Colombia report sexual violence to the authorities, according to the viewpoint?

Amnesty International, "Colombian Authorities Fail to Stop or Punish Sexual Violence Against Women," October 4, 2012. Reproduced with permission.

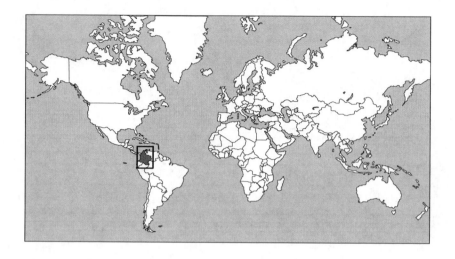

3. What is the legal framework for peace, and how could it hurt an investigation of sexual violence, according to Amnesty International?

The Colombian authorities have failed to make real progress in bringing to justice those responsible for conflict-related sexual crimes, said Amnesty International in a new report today [October 4, 2012].

No Consequences

The report "Colombia: Hidden from Justice: Impunity for Conflict-Related Sexual Violence, a Follow-Up Report" examines efforts made by the authorities over the past year to ensure those suspected of criminal responsibility for sexual violence in the country's long-running armed conflict face justice.

"By failing to investigate effectively sexual violence against women, the Colombian authorities are sending a dangerous message to perpetrators that they can continue to rape and sexually abuse without fear of the consequences," said Marcelo Pollack, Colombia researcher at Amnesty International.

"Respect for human rights must be at the top of the agenda in the forthcoming peace talks between the government and the Revolutionary Armed Forces of Colombia (FARC). Without a clear commitment from all the parties to the conflict to end sexual violence and other human rights abuses there can be no lasting and stable peace in Colombia."

In the context of Colombia's armed conflict, women are targets of sexual violence to sow terror within communities to force them to flee their land, wreak revenge on the enemy, control the sexual and reproductive rights of female combatants or exploit women and girls as sexual slaves.

An increasing number of women human rights activists working to denounce and fight abuses have themselves been targets of threats and attacks.

"Without a clear commitment from all the parties to the conflict to end sexual violence and other human rights abuses there can be no lasting and stable peace in Colombia."

Afraid to Speak

Sexual violence, particularly in the context of the conflict, is often not reported to the authorities as women are frequently too scared to talk, fear the stigmatization attached to being a survivor of sexual violence or believe the crime will not be effectively investigated.

Obstacles to justice include a lack of effective security for survivors and for those involved in legal proceedings; discrimination and stigmatization of women survivors by judicial officials; and the lack of a comprehensive strategy to combat impunity in such cases. Bureaucratic inefficiencies, underfunding and the infiltration of local state institutions by illegal armed groups also impede the ability of the civilian justice system to deliver justice.

"The problem in Colombia has not primarily been the lack of relatively good laws, resolutions, decrees, protocols and directives, these exist in abundance, but rather the failure to implement them effectively and consistently across the country," said Pollack.

A number of high-level officials—including Vice President Angelino Garzón and the attorney general—have publicly expressed their commitment to find justice for the survivors of conflict-related sexual violence.

Several legislative initiatives have also been presented over the past year that could, if implemented effectively, have a positive impact with regard to victims' rights to truth, justice and reparation.

Earlier this year, Colombian legislators Iván Cepeda and Ángela María Robledo, with the support of Pilar Rueda, the human rights ombudsman's delegate for children, youth and women, presented a legislative bill in Congress to combat impunity in cases of conflict-related sexual crimes.

"The only way of ending sexual violence against women and girls in Colombia is by ensuring that those suspected of criminal responsibility face justice."

If approved, this legislation will, among other things, amend the criminal code to reflect international standards by making conflict-related sexual violence a specific criminal offence under national law.

A number of legislative projects, however, threaten to undermine further efforts to bring to justice those suspected of responsibility for crimes under international law.

One of the bills currently being debated in Congress will strengthen the military justice system's role in investigating and prosecuting crimes under international law in which members of the security forces are implicated. Although the proposed law states that conflict-related sexual crimes are excluded from military jurisdiction, it gives the military justice system greater control over the initial and, therefore, crucial stage of the investigation.

Another legislative initiative, known as the "legal framework for peace," was passed by Congress in June 2012 and was signed into law by President [Juan Manuel] Santos [Calderón] soon after. The law could allow human rights abusers, including members of the security forces, to benefit from de facto amnesties. It will give Congress the power to suspend the prison sentences of members of the warring parties, including of the security forces.

"The only way of ending sexual violence against women and girls in Colombia is by ensuring that those suspected of criminal responsibility face justice," said Pollack.

"If Colombia continues to be unable or unwilling genuinely to bring to justice those responsible for conflict-related sexual crimes, then this could require the International Criminal Court to step in."

Amnesty International called on the Colombian authorities to develop and implement an effective, comprehensive interdisciplinary plan of action to address sexual violence against women and to support the bill before Congress "to guarantee access to justice for victims of sexual violence, especially sexual violence in the context of the armed conflict."

Sexual Violence Directed Against Men in Wartime Is Underreported and Under-Analyzed

Maite Vermeulen

Maite Vermeulen is a Dutch journalist. In the following viewpoint, she argues that sexual violence against men in wartime is often ignored or minimized. She says that men are generally not considered to be victims of sexual violence and are often very reluctant to report such acts. Nonetheless, she says, sexual violence against men for purposes of intimidation, genocide, or torture is widespread and can take many forms. She concludes that the international community must do more to investigate sexual violence against men in wartime and to treat all victims equally, regardless of gender.

As you read, consider the following questions:

1. Besides anal rape, what other forms does Vermeulen say that sexual violence against men can take?

2. What evidence does Vermeulen provide to show that NGOs largely ignore the issue of male sexual violence?

3. What kinds of future research into sexual violence against men does Vermeulen suggest?

Maite Vermeulen, "Hidden Victims: The Story of Sexual Violence Against Men in Conflict," e-International Relations, September 4, 2011. Reproduced with permission.

As early as the ancient Persians, sexual violence against men and boys has been part of warfare. Murals from this period show the victors of battle parading with plates stacked high with their enemies' penises. This practice of emasculating the enemy is today still an integral part of armed conflict. Indeed, as [A.] DelZotto and [A.] Jones write, 'what greater humiliation can one man impose on another man or boy than to turn him into a de facto "female" through sexual cruelty?'

A Wall of Silence

Over time, however, the topic of sexual violence against men has become a taboo in society, as the homophobic visions of Judaism, Christianity and Islam became institutionalised. Nonetheless, male sexual violence in conflict settings still exists. The culture of impunity in war-torn societies fosters the use of these brutal tactics to obtain military and political goals.

Sexual violence against women has become a prominent issue in political, humanitarian, legal, and academic spheres in the past two decades. Sexualised violence against men, on the other hand, is still surrounded by 'a wall of silence' [according to DelZotto and Jones]. Breaking down this wall, and treating the issue alongside sexual violence against women, is important to help these hidden victims of war, as well as to punish the perpetrators.

Typical of the discourse surrounding sexual violence is the use of the term in such a way as to signal violence against women only. It is moreover wrongly used synonymously with the concept of gender-based violence. The World Health Organization, for instance, states on its website that 'gender-based violence, or violence against women (VAW), is a major public health and human rights problem'. This is, however, not how these terms shall be used in this [viewpoint]. Whereas gender-based violence will be defined as 'violence that is targeted at women or men because of their sex and/or their socially constructed gender roles' [according to C. Carpenter], sexual violence is 'any violence, whether physical and/or mental, carried out through sexual means or by targeting sexuality' [as stated by D.A. Lewis]. Both terms can, and should, hence be used to signify violence against both men and women. Sexual violence is a part of gender-based violence, alongside such phenomena as forced conscription and sex-selective massacre.

This [viewpoint] will explore why the discourse on wartime sexual violence only revolves around women and why men's experience of sexual violence is largely ignored. First, the different forms of sexual violence against men, the scope of the problem and the dynamics that drive the violence will be sketched. Then, the three aspects of the neglect will be discussed in turn: the under-reporting of the issue, relating to victim's experience; the under-recognition, describing the discourse in the international community in both policy, humanitarian and scholarly circles; and the under-punishment, exploring the gaps in the international law system. It will be concluded that a change of mind-set is necessary to bring sexual violence against men in armed conflict to the forefront of political, humanitarian, legal and scholarly discussion to give support and justice to the victims.

Wartime Sexual Violence Against Men

Sexual violence against men is surrounded by misinformation and misunderstanding. Many social and health workers are only familiar with sexual violence against women, which often is rape. Harry Van Tienhoven, working in the refugee health care centre in Utrecht, The Netherlands, has described how these "experts" hence assume that sexual violence against men takes the same form, that is anal rape.

Anal rape is, however, only one of many forms of sexual violence against men. Victims may be forced to perform fellatio on the perpetrators or other victims, or may be anally raped using objects. They may also be forced to rape other victims, including family members or the dead. This has been called 'enforced rape', or 'forced incest', and has been reported in Sierra Leone, among other conflicts. There is also the concept of 'rape plus', the plus signifying infection with HIV/AIDS, which has been documented in Kosovo.

Enforced sterilisation is another type of sexual violence. It has been extensively documented in the war in former Yugoslavia, where eyewitnesses and victims have reported castration through brutal means: 'I saw how Muslims were forced to bite each other's testicles off, their mouth filled with testicles and blood' [according to the International Criminal Tribunal for the Former Yugoslavia].

Other kinds of sexual violence against men include sexual slavery, as happened in Liberia, and forced masturbation of the captors, which was documented in Sri Lanka. The infamous Abu Ghraib case in Iraq showed victims forced to undress, while being sexually threatened. There are also numerous examples of genital violence in such conflicts as Croatia, Sri Lanka and Northern Ireland, like amputation of the penis and electroshock or beatings to the testicles.

Anal rape is . . . only one of many forms of sexual violence against men.

The variety of countries named in the above section exemplifies that sexual violence against men is not limited to a certain type of conflict or culture. Wynne Russell states that sexual violence against men and boys has been reported in 25 armed conflicts around the world. If the sexual exploitation of boys displaced by conflict is taken into account, the vast majority of the 59 armed conflicts listed in the 2007 human security report qualify.

The scarce academic literature on the topic consistently points to the lack of exact numbers regarding the scale of the violence, as most evidence is anecdotal. Yet the academics who identify this gap in research have hitherto failed to fill it. Nonetheless, a number of estimates have been made, some based on peacetime statistics, others based on research in post-conflict areas.

Peacetime sexual violence against men is not a perfect equivalent of sexual violence in wartime, yet as Lewis points out, it may shed some light upon the scope of the problem. One researcher found that in a general household sample in the United States (US), 7.2% of men had experienced some kind of sexual assault. An analysis of 120 US incidence studies of rape showed that 3% of men and 13% of women have been raped in their lifetime.

A more relevant quantitative study to assess the scale of sexual violence against men in armed conflict can be found in the research by [K.] Johnson et al., undertaken in post-conflict Liberia. They found that among former combatants, 42.3% of females and 32.6% of males had experienced sexual violence, compared to 9.2% and 7.4% among non-combatants respectively.

The most telling data are taken from the war in the former Yugoslavia, as the trials before the International Criminal Tribunal for the Former Yugoslavia (ICTY) prompted the first thorough research into sexual violence in armed conflict, including sexual violence against men. In one assessment of a concentration camp in Sarajevo Canton, 80% of the 5,000 male prisoners reported having been raped. . . .

Dynamics of Sexual Violence

Sexual violence in armed conflict can be explained through a number of interlinked rationales. In some cases, it is arbitrary—a result of the breakdown of social and legal frameworks. In others, especially when targeted against women, it may be used for personal gratification, military training or rewarding of soldiers. In most cases, however, it is a systematic weapon of war—used to further political or military goals, which may include displacing populations, eliciting information or ethnic cleansing.

The dynamics underlying the use of sexual violence as a war tactic are twofold: They rely on structures of power and dominance and processes of emasculation of the individual and the group. Ruth Seifert, in her analysis of rape makes the important point that 'in the act of rape the perpetrator's sexuality is not an end in itself. Rather, it is used as an instrument in exerting violence'. Indeed, sexual violence is all about power and dominance over the victim. Female rape can be seen as a form of male-to-male communication, stressing how men fail to protect their women from harm, thereby dominating them. When men are made to watch sexual violence against their female relatives, this secondary victimisation is particularly effective.

The male victim is tainted with feminine and/or homosexual characteristics.

This communication is arguably even more invasive when men themselves are the subject of sexual violence. Men are considered to represent strength and power, able to protect others. Hence, male sexual violence both empowers the masculinity of the perpetrator and disempowers the victim and his community. Especially when the violence is performed in public, this may spread fear in the community.

For male victims of sexual violence, their masculinity and their victimisation are incompatible. Hence, they are emasculated, no "real men" anymore, because "real men" would have resisted the attack. The male victim is tainted with feminine and/or homosexual characteristics, which may have even greater significance in times of conflict, when constructs of

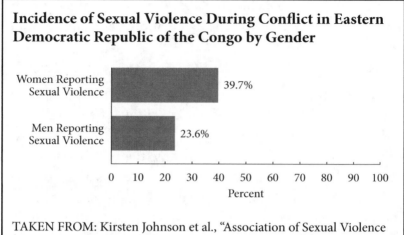

Incidence of Sexual Violence During Conflict in Eastern Democratic Republic of the Congo by Gender

Women Reporting Sexual Violence — 39.7%

Men Reporting Sexual Violence — 23.6%

Percent

TAKEN FROM: Kirsten Johnson et al., "Association of Sexual Violence and Human Rights Violations with Physical and Mental Health in Territories of the Eastern Democratic Republic of the Congo," *JAMA,* vol. 304, no. 5, August 4, 2010. www.ncbi.nlm.nih.gov.

masculinity are more pronounced. Ironically, these feminine/ homosexual attributes only adhere to the victim, while the attacker is viewed as more masculine through his domination.

Prevention of procreation through enforced sterilisation may further add to the emasculation of the victim and the entire community. It may be used for ethnic cleansing, as happened in the former Yugoslavia, where only men were seen to carry ethnicity. One man testified before the International Court of Justice that 'they [Serb torturers] were deliberately aiming their beatings at our testicles saying "you'll never make Muslim children again"'. Indeed, sexual violence is more prevalent in conflicts of identity.

The effects of male sexual violence on the victim break down into physical problems, including sexually transmitted infections and impotence; psychosomatic problems, such as sleeplessness, anxiety, deep feelings of shame and guilt, suicidal thoughts and post-traumatic stress disorder; and psychosocial problems, like marital stress and drug or alcohol abuse.

Victims may also start to doubt their sexual orientation, as they may have had an erection or ejaculated during the assault.

Under-Reporting—The Victims

Having established the forms, scale and dynamics of wartime sexual violence against men, the taboo surrounding it will now be further analysed. The aforementioned lack of data on the prevalence results from a large-scale under-reporting on the part of the victims. In a survey of 40 sexually abused men in the United Kingdom, only 5 men had reported their assault to the police. A combination of shame, confusion, guilt, fear and stigma contribute to this under-reporting. Men feel they should cope "like a man". This applies in peacetime, and possibly even more strongly in wartime, when, as S. Sivakumaran points out, 'men tend to self-identify with masculine stereotypes more strongly'. As mentioned above, the strong image of masculinity and the weak image of victimisation are in contrast.

English is 'bereft of terms and phrases which accurately describe male rape'.

Moreover, the victim may struggle with, what Sivakumaran dubs a "taint" of homosexuality attached to male/male rape. Combined with societal stigmatisation, this causes a further disincentive to report the crime. Especially in armed conflicts, to cast this emasculating "taint" may be the intention of the perpetrator. To further complicate this scenario, homosexual activity, regardless of consent, is illegal in many countries, such as Zimbabwe and may even attract the death penalty, like proposed in Uganda.

These stereotypes are not the only hindrance for the reporting of male sexual violence. Victims may also be unable to find the right words to express themselves. As R.J. Mc-

Mullen writes, English is 'bereft of terms and phrases which accurately describe male rape'.

The final point to take into account here is the crude fact that many victims die from the consequences of the assault, and their remains may not show signs of sexual violence. . . .

Not all victims of sexual violence [have] received equal consideration. The political attention of the West has only been focused on certain groups of female victims, most notably those in the Balkan and the Middle East. Indeed, the [George W.] Bush administration framed the war against the Taliban regime in Afghanistan in 2001 as a war 'against people who are mean to women' [states John Zogby, an American writer]. It is unsurprising then that men are excluded as a potential group of victims by these political elites, who have a 'highly gendered understanding of who is to be secured' [according to Carpenter]. Exemplary of this exclusion are the asylum policies of Western countries. When DelZotto and Jones examined 36 US asylum cases of women versus 44 cases of men, they found that all but two women were asked whether or not they would face sexual danger in their country of origin, whereas none of the men were asked equivalent questions.

Many health care and social workers are not sufficiently trained to recognise the signs of sexual assault in men.

The strategic motives may explain why political elites do not recognise wartime sexual violence against men as a serious problem, yet the question remains why, in humanitarian circles, NGOs [nongovernmental organisations] also still largely ignore the issue. DelZotto and Jones identify that there are 4,076 NGOs that address war rape and sexual violence. Yet only 3% of those mention men in their literature, and a quarter explicitly deny that sexual violence against men is a serious problem. It has been argued that NGOs are highly politicised, with many of these organisations relying on governments and private enterprises for the majority of their funding. Hence, their agendas need to be in line with the agendas of the political elites.

Another reason for this lack of grassroots action to support male victims of sexual violence in conflict regions is that many health care and social workers are not sufficiently trained to recognise the signs of sexual assault in men. The stereotype that sexual violence can only be inflicted on women also influences these workers, and many types of sexual violence do not leave permanent visible damage. Moreover, health care workers may classify what happened to their patients as 'torture' or 'abuse', failing to provide sufficient counselling and recognition of the underlying problems.

Finally, with stereotyping and ignorance characterising the political and humanitarian discourse, the scholarly sphere does not fare much better. Some key scholars on the issue of rape warfare plainly exclude men as possible victims, thus reinforcing the stereotypes underlying the very problem. Others mention the possibility of male victims in passing, and many excuse themselves from exploring the topic further by pointing out the lack of data. There are, however, some exceptions, most notably Sivakumaran, who explored the issue of male sexual violence in armed conflict thoroughly though by no means exhaustively. . . .

Some key scholars on the issue of rape warfare plainly exclude men as possible victims.

The 2001 [Dusko] Tadic case before the ICTY saw the first international conviction regarding sexual violence against men in armed conflict. An analysis of the sentencing patterns at the ICTY, however, shows that sexual violence against men has been punished less severely than similar violence against women.

The prosecution of perpetrators of male sexual violence in wartime is thus not straightforward. The consequential climate of impunity has, according to some authors, contributed to its becoming "epidemic". In the same line of thought, Lewis concludes that 'explicit recognition in international instruments would [. . .] put potential perpetrators on notice that sexual violence against men is just as serious a crime as it is against women'. Indeed, the importance of providing recognition and justice to male victims of sexual violence in armed conflict cannot be overstated. Yet to say that perpetrators—rebels and combatants on the ground—consider the possibility of being prosecuted under international law seems unrealistic.

[This viewpoint] argues for a more equal treatment of all categories of victims.

Treating All Victims Equally

Sexual violence is arguably one of the worst types of violence, targeting a person's identity, as well as the identity of his or her group. The psychological consequences often far outlive those of other forms of violence. Progress has been made to address wartime sexual violence against women, yet men remain a hidden category of victims. This is caused by a combination of under-reporting on the side of the victims, under-recognition by politicians, humanitarian workers and academics, and under-punishment through gaps in the international legal system.

This [viewpoint] has by no means tried to downplay the severity of the issue of sexual violence against women, nor against any other vulnerable group. It rather argues for a more equal treatment of all categories of victims. The exposure of male-directed sexual violence in conflict will help to emphasise the broader phenomenon of sexual violence against women and girls, for what it really is: 'not "boys being boys" but an exercise in power and humiliation' [according to W. Russell].

Discussion

The scant literature that identifies the problem of male sexual violence in wartime has not researched any broader implications of the phenomenon, nor has this [viewpoint] for a lack of space and resources. Future research could focus on the impact of male sexual violence on post-conflict reintegration of combatants and civilian men forced to rape relatives; its contribution to such practices as prostitution, survival sex or human trafficking; and its effect on the incidence of sexual violence against women and children, including refugees and child soldiers. Moreover, it has not yet been established whether the needs of survivors differ between the sexes. Research into the kind of treatment that would benefit male victims of sexual violence has hitherto been scarce and only focused on peacetime situations. It is important to be aware that all of these issues need to be addressed without unintentionally reinforcing existing stereotypes of gender roles and homosexuality, which underlie the violence in the first place.

Surviving Rape in Iran's Prisons: Introduction

Iran Human Rights Documentation Center

The Iran Human Rights Documentation Center (IHRDC) is an independent nonprofit organization that seeks to create a comprehensive and objective historical record of the human rights situation in Iran. In the following viewpoint, IHRDC reports on the long-standing use of rape as a form of torture, terror, and coercion in Iranian prisons. IHRDC says that rape was used against political opponents from the Iranian revolution in 1979 and is still used against dissidents and protestors.

As you read, consider the following questions:

1. According to IHRDC, what are the two reasons that rape victims are unwilling to speak about their experiences?

2. Why does IHRDC say that Iranian guards would force virgin girls into temporary marriages before executing them?

3. Who was Hojatol-Eslam Haj-Agha Khaleghi, and what happened to him, according to IHRDC?

Introduction

Allegations of rape and sexual violence of political prisoners by authorities began to emerge after the Islamic Republic of

Iran Human Rights Documentation Center, "Introduction," *Surviving Rape in Iran's Prisons*, June 2011. Reproduced with permission.

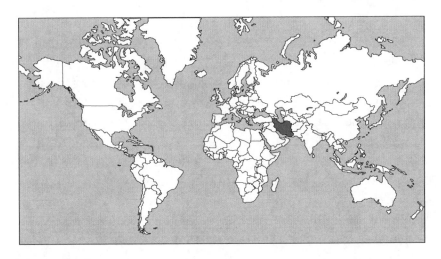

Iran was established in 1979 and have continued, to varying degrees, to the present. However, not surprisingly, there is no reliable estimate of the number of prisoners raped in the Islamic Republic's prisons; no data or comprehensive report has ever been compiled that portrays the full scope of sexual violence in Iran's prisons. The reasons are simple: Few rape victims are willing to speak about their experiences due to (1) government pressure and acquiescence, and (2) social stigma. Iranian authorities have and continue to acquiesce to rapes of prisoners by guards and interrogators who use rape to crush detainees' spirits, inflict humiliation, discourage their dissent, force them to confess to crimes, and ultimately to intimidate them and others.

Rape is always traumatic and has long-term physical, psychological and social effects on victims. Understandably, this means that many victims are unable to publicly acknowledge their experiences, even many years later.[1] Many have never even told their families. Given these circumstances, therefore, it is very likely that the few witnesses who have come forward

1. See Golnaz Esfandiari, *New prison rape allegations in Iran bring practice to light*, RADIO FREE EUROPE, Aug. 26, 2009, *available at* http://www.rferl.org/articleprintview /1808311.html (last visited June 3, 2011).

to report rapes they witnessed and experienced in Iranian prisons represent only a small percentage of the total number of cases.

This report documents the ordeals of five former prisoners—two women and three men. They span the almost 30 years of the Islamic Republic's existence. Four witnesses were raped; one was threatened with rape and saw rape victims. Three of the rape victims were politically active, one in the early days of the revolution and the other two during the last few years. All experienced overtly violent and gang rape. In addition to being gang-raped, one of the victims was sexually exploited by a guard. All were traumatized, and some considered suicide.

Many victims are unable to publicly acknowledge their experiences, even many years later.

IHRDC has interviewed many former prisoners who were raped or threatened with rape in Iranian prisons. While many chose to not tell their stories publicly, we wish to express our heartfelt understanding and thank you to all who agreed to speak with us about their experiences.

I. Rape and Sexual Abuse in Iran's Prisons Since 1979

Numerous reports of rape and sexual violence of detainees by Iranian authorities surfaced after the June 12, 2009, presidential election.[2] For example, a teenager using the name "Ardeshir" described his detention in an unofficial detention center where he was repeatedly raped and watched others be-

---

2. See IRAN HUMAN RIGHTS DOCUMENTATION CENTER (IHRDC), VIOLENT AFTERMATH: THE 2009 ELECTION AND SUPPRESSION OF DISSENT IN IRAN 47-48 (2010), *available at* http://www.iranhrdc.org/english/publications/reports/3161-violent-aftermath-the-2009-election-and-suppression-of-dissent-in-iran.html [hereinafter VIOLENT AFTERMATH].

ing taken from cells to be raped.[3] A young woman using the name "Sara" reported being repeatedly raped by her interrogator after refusing to disclose the whereabouts of her brother. She reported that her interrogator raped her "from top to bottom" and "stuck up his arm deep into her body." She was forced to falsely confess to having sexual intercourse with her brother. Her interrogator continued to summon and rape her after her release from prison.[4]

A teenager using the name "Reza" told of his arrest with 40 other boys during an opposition demonstration in a "large provincial city." Reza was raped as the other boys watched. After he reported the rape to his interrogator, his interrogator raped him so he would learn not to tell such tales anywhere else.[5] An alleged former *Basij* member reported that rape of detainees was a reward conferred on Iranian Revolutionary Guard Corps (*Sepah-e Pasdaran-e Enqelab-e Eslami* or *Sepah*) and *Basij* members for crushing the demonstrations. He told how he and a relative came to realize that *Basij* members were raping children who had been arrested. When his relative confronted the senior officer, he "calmly replied with a smile: 'This is *Fath Al Moin* [aid to victory]. It's a worthy deed. There's nothing wrong with it. Why are you complaining?'"[6]

It soon became public that many demonstrators were detained and severely mistreated at the Kahrizak Detention Center outside Tehran. A former detainee reported hearing screams of younger and quieter detainees being raped. Mehdi Karroubi, a former speaker of the *Majlis*, and a presidential

3. Martin Fletcher and Special Correspondent in Tehran, *Raped and beaten for daring to question President Ahmadinejad's election*, THE TIMES, Sept. 11, 2009, *available at* http://www.timesonline.co.uk/tol/news/world/middle_east/article6829921.ece.

4. HUMAN RIGHTS & DEMOCRACY LIBRARY, Boroumand Foundation Interview of "Sara," *available at* http://www.iranrights.org/english/document-1512.php.

5. Homa Homayoun, *Iranian boy who defied Tehran hardliners tells of prison rape ordeal*, THE TIMES, Aug. 22, 2009, *available at* http://www.timesonline.co.uk/tol/news/world/middle_east/article6805885.ece.

6. Lindsey Hilsum, *Iran militia man, 'I hope God forgives me,'* Dec. 16, 2009, *available at* http://www.channel4.com/news/iran-militia-man-i-hope-god-forgives-me.

candidate in 2009, published a letter to Ayatollah Rafsanjani, then head of the Expediency Council, alleging torture and sexual abuse of post-election detainees, and the regime closed the facility.[7] However, as noted by the Iranian lawyer Shadi Sadr, this wave of rapes was not an "incident." It was a continuation of practices that had existed since the 1979 revolution.[8]

A former detainee reported hearing screams of younger and quieter detainees being raped.

During the early days after the revolution, many young men and women were imprisoned for political activities, and/or being members of ethnic or religious minorities, and charged with minor offenses.[9] There were reports of interrogators raping and sexually molesting prisoners. For example, Amnesty International reported the rape of a girl in a solitary cell by *Sepah* members in 1982. Amnesty reported that "she was forced to undress and submit to oral and anal sex. She was virgin."[10]

Beginning in 1985, United Nations special representatives to Iran issued regular reports documenting allegations of

---

7. See VIOLENT AFTERMATH, supra note 2, at 51; Letter from Mehdi Karroubi to Ayatollah Hashemi Rafsanjani, Head of the Expediency Council (July 31, 2009), English translation *available at* http://khordaad88.com/?p=75.

8. Shadi Sadr, *Feminist Attorney Speaks Out Against Rape As a Weapon of Torture in Iran [translated by Frieda Afary]*, PAYVAND IRAN NEWS, Sept. 8, 2009, *available at* http://www.payvand.com/news/09/sep/1080.html.

9. See AYATOLLAH HOSSEIN-ALI MONTAZERI, KHATIRAT-I AYATOLLAH MONTAZERI, MAJMU'IYYIH PAYVASTHA VA DASTNIVISHA [MEMOIR OF AYATOLLAH MONTAZERI, THE COLLECTION OF APPENDICES AND HANDWRITTEN NOTES] 585 (2001) [hereinafter MONTAZERI'S MEMOIRS].

10. Amnesty International, *Newsletter*, Apr. 1985, vol. XV, No. 4, *available at* http://www.iranrights.org/english/document-105-316.php. Over the years since, former prisoners have spoken of rape in prison. See, e.g., PARVIN PAIDAR, WOMEN AND THE POLITICAL PROCESS IN TWENTIETH-CENTURY IRAN 347 (1995); Nasrin Parvaz, *Zireh Boteh Lala Abasi, [Under the Magnolia Bush]* Chapter 10, at 1 (2002), *available at* http://www.nasrinparvaz.com/Book/10.htm; Reza Allamehzadeh, Video Interview of Nina Aghdam, *Are, Halem Khoba . . . [Yes, I'm fine . . .]*, *available at* http://www.youtube.com/watch?v=_vTM3MyzcsM&NR=1.

sexual violence and rape in prisons. In a 1987 report, the special representative noted that six sympathizers of the People's Mojahedin Organization of Iran testified about experiencing and witnessing many forms of torture, including sexual abuse, in Iranian prisons.[11] One woman, Mina Vatani, reported that she witnessed seventy persons being executed in Evin Prison in early 1982, and that the victims included pregnant women and women who had been raped before being executed.[12] The special representative also reported that three of the witnesses were examined by Dr. Claudine Jeannet of Geneva in 1986. Dr. Jeannet certified that as a result of being raped, a woman named Azame had many "serious infections that required the removal of her appendix and uterus and an operation on her left ovary."[13]

In his 1988 and 1989 reports, the special representative reported witness testimony that prison authorities had raped prisoners.[14] In 1988, the representative held informal hearings at which sixteen former prisoners testified about their knowledge and experiences of prison conditions and torture, including rape. Seven were Bahá'is and nine "described themselves as sympathizers of the Mojahedin organization."[15] One witness testified that a woman in her sixties was raped and executed; another stated that she witnessed revolutionary guards

11. U.N. Econ. & Soc. Council [ECOSOC], Commission on Human Rights, *Report on the human rights situation in the Islamic Republic of Iran by the Special Representative of the Commission, Mr. Reynaldo Galindo Pohl*, ¶ 50, U.N. Doc. E/CN.4/1987/23 (Jan. 28, 1987) [hereinafter Galindo Pohl Report 1987].
12. Id. ¶ 47(a).
13. Id. ¶ 51(a).
14. ECOSOC, Commission on Human Rights, *Report on the human rights situation in the Islamic Republic of Iran by the Special Representative of the Commission, Mr. Reynaldo Galindo Pohl*, ¶ 9, U.N. Doc. E/CN.4/1988/24 (Jan. 25, 1988), [hereinafter Galindo Pohl Report 1988]; U.N. General Assembly, *Report of the Economic and Social Council, Situation of human rights in the Islamic Republic of Iran, Note by the Secretary-General*, ¶78, U.N. Doc. A/44/620 (Nov. 2, 1989), [hereinafter Secretary-General Note 1989].
15. U.N. General Assembly, *Report of the Economic and Social Council, Situation of human rights in the Islamic Republic of Iran, Note by the Secretary-General*, ¶¶ 12-16, U.N. Doc. A/43/705 (Oct. 13, 1988), [hereinafter Secretary-General Note 1988].

raping girls.[16] There were also reports of threats of sexual abuse made to female prisoners and female relatives of male prisoners.[17] The 1989 report described the testimony of Shahrzad Alavi Shahidi who reported that a female prisoner became mad after suffering torture and rape. The authorities did not provide physical or psychological care, and she committed suicide in prison.[18]

Witnesses also told the special representative that government authorities had given families of several executed female political prisoners certificates of marriage of their executed relatives. The certificates allegedly indicated that the prisoners had been raped before execution.[19] Many have similarly reported that virgin girls sentenced to execution were forced into temporary marriages with prison guards because the guards believed young girls executed while virgins would go to heaven.[20] Once married, the guards raped the girls to prevent them from going to heaven.[21] It has also been reported that,

16. Id. ¶¶14 and 16.
17. Id. ¶34
18. Secretary-General Note 1989, *supra* note 14, ¶ 34.
19. Id. ¶ 27.
20. Temporary marriage in Iran (*siqih* or *nikah-i munqati'*) is a legal contract between a man (married or not) and an unmarried woman. At the time of marriage, the woman must be an unmarried virgin, divorced or widowed. In the contract, both parties agree on the time period for the relationship and the bride gift (*mihriyyih*) to be paid to the woman. A man can marry as many women as he wants through temporary marriage. A woman cannot be involved in more than one temporary marriage at once, and cannot enter into a new temporary marriage before completing a waiting period mandated by law. *See Ahkam-i Siqih [Laws of Temporary Marriage] under Ahkam-i Nikah [Laws of Marriage], RISALIHYIH IMAM KHOMEINI, available at* http://takteb.ir/articles/45-islam/298-ahkam.html.
21. See Galindo Pohl Report 1987, *supra* note 11; MARINA NEMAT, PRISONER OF TEHRAN 101 (2007); Shahrnush Parsipur, *Zindani Tehrah [Tehran Prisoner], a Critique of Tehran Prisoner by Marina Nemat*, RADIO ZAMANEH, Feb. 25, 2009, *available at* http://zamaaneh.com/parsipur/2009/02/post_234.html (last visited June 6, 2011); Alahi Shad interview with Soudabeh Ardavan, *Ba doxtaran adami tajavez mishod ke ba behesht naravand, [Girls Sentenced to Execution were Raped to Deny Them Heaven]*, RADIO FARDA, Aug. 16, 2009, [hereinafter Shad interview with Ardavan], *available at* http://www.radiofarda.com/content/F7_Soudabeh_Ardavan_IV _on_Torture_in_Iran_Prisons/1800927.html (last visited June 6, 2011), Nasrin Parvaz, *Zindan idama darad v man az "tavabin" dafa mikonem [Prison Continues and I "Defend" the Repentant]*, Aug. 4, 2007, *available at* http://www.nasrinparvaz.com/M /Marina%20Nemat.htm.

on some occasions, the authorities sent families money and sweets with the bodies of executed female prisoners.[22]

The regular use of sexual violence and rape in Iranian prisons was confirmed in a 1986 letter to Supreme Leader Ayatollah Ruhollah Khomeini from his designated successor Ayatollah Hossein Ali Montazeri:

> Do you know that in the Islamic Republic prisons, young girls are possessed by force? Do you know that it is a common practice to abuse girls with foul languages during interrogations? Do you know that there are many prisoners, who have been blinded, deafened, paralyzed or suffer from serious pains due to inhuman treatments and nobody addresses their plight?[23]

However, reports of rape by interrogators and guards continued. In 1990, the special representative continued to report that "a virgin woman condemned to death goes through forced matrimony and is deflowered before the death sentence is carried out."[24] Navab-Ali Ghaem-Maghami was reported to have been sexually molested by the authorities in Ghom prison, and forced to watch other prisoners being tortured. His clothes were allegedly soiled with urine and excrement from other prisoners.[25] Mehrangiz Yeganeh was repeatedly and brutally raped while serving two and a half years in Tabriz prison. The rapes caused damage to her intestines requiring surgery.[26] A male prisoner was allegedly forced to perform sexual acts and another was sexually abused by four prison guards.[27]

---

22. See IRAN BRIEFING, *Female Prisoners Raped Before Execution "Lest They Go To Paradise,"* Aug. 26, 2010, *available at* http://iranbriefing.net/?p=62; Shad interview with Ardavan, *supra* note 20.

23. MONTAZERI'S MEMOIRS, *supra* note 9, at 586-587; REZA AFSHARI, HUMAN RIGHTS IN IRAN, THE ABUSE OF CULTURAL RELATIVISM 105 (2001).

24. U.N. General Assembly, *Report of the Economic and Social Council, Situation of human rights in the Islamic Republic of Iran, Note by the Secretary-General,* ¶ 82, U.N. Doc. A/45/697 (Nov. 6, 1990) [hereinafter Secretary-General Note 1990].

25. Id. ¶ 55(k).

26. Id. ¶ 55(y).

27. Id. ¶¶ 55(s) and (u).

In 1991, a former prisoner told the special representative that he had witnessed investigators raping young women.[28] In 1992, the representative reported that the head of Ghazvin prison and a religious judge, Hojatol-Eslam Haj-Agha Khaleghi, was alleged to have made sexual advances to female prisoners and if they resisted, subject them to torture and rape. He was arrested but released after a short time and continued to work as an interrogator at the prison.[29]

Do you know that in the Islamic Republic prisons, young girls are possessed by force?

Beginning in 1999, imprisoned journalists, bloggers, and students reported that interrogators raped and threatened them with rape.[30] Prisoners were also threatened with arrest and rape of their family members unless they confessed. For example, Ahmad Batebi, featured on the cover of the July 13, 1999, issue of the *Economist* participating in a student demonstration, wrote in a public letter that, "[d]uring the interrogations, they threatened several times to execute me and to torture and rape my family members as well as imprison them for long terms."[31]

---

28. Id. ¶ 129.
29. ECOSOC, Commission on Human Rights, *Report on the human rights situation in the Islamic Republic of Iran by the Special Representative of the Commission on Human Rights, Mr. Reynaldo Galindo Pohl*, ¶ 134, U.N. Doc. E/CN.4/1992/34 (Jan. 2, 1992) [hereinafter Galindo Pohl Report 1992].
30. See Amnesty International, *Iran: Five Years of injustice and ill treatment: Akbar Mohammadi-Case Sheet*, July 7, 2004, AI Index MDE 13/027/2004, *available at* http://www.unhcr.org/refworld/pdfid/42ae98bd0.pdf ("in 2000 and 2001 former students who arrived in European countries seeking asylum were able to seek treatment for incidences of torture—including instrumental rape carried out on men—that were allegedly carried out by officials during and after the July 1999 events of 18 Tir").
31. *Public letter of Ahmad Batebi (Hero of the Economist) to the special investigation team of the Islamic judiciary, Mar. 23, 2000*, English translation *available at*, http://www.iranrights.org/english/document-201-392.php.

Omid Memarian, a journalist and blogger, was arrested in 2004 and spent six and a half months in detention. He reported that his interrogator

> [u]sed very graphic sexual language during the interrogation process. He often called me "pretty boy." Sometimes he played with my face, or grabbed my cheeks and ears, or gently brushed my arms and shoulders with his hands. When he did these things, I became extremely worried. I thought he would do something to me. As he did these things he would tell me, in graphic fashion, what he wanted from me. When he explained these things, I often began to cry. I felt horrible. I was in a room alone with a fifty-five-year-old man, discussing sexual issues which I could not even discuss with my closest friends.[32]

While transferring Memarian to Evin prison, a guard warned: "God willing, they will eventually make a groom out of you." Memarian remembers that he "knew there is a history of rape in Iran's prisons," and therefore "did not doubt the fact that they were capable of doing such things."[33] Ali Afshari, a student leader in Iran, had similar experiences after he was arrested for the third time in early 2000. His interrogator whispered in his ear that he would be raped if he did not confess, and then described how it would be done by inserting a bottle in his anus.[34]

"Mahdis," a young woman arrested in 2002 following a student protest and held in Evin prison, reported that she was repeatedly raped by her interrogators:

> Following my second interrogation, I was raped for three days. I was bleeding, but they did not even give me a pad. They raped me in a violent manner. The two men never

32. IHRDC, FORCED CONFESSIONS: TARGETING IRAN'S CYBER-JOURNALISTS 31 (2009), *available at* http://www.iranhrdc.org/english/publications/reports/3159-forced-confessions-targeting-iran-s-cyber-journalists.html.
33. Id.
34. IHRDC, Witness Statement of Ali Afshari, at 13, *available at* http://www.iranhrdc.org/english/publications/witness-testimony/3175-witness-statement-ali-afshari.html.

said their names. They called each other "Seyyed" or "Haji." The first time, I begged them not to rape me and I told them that I was a virgin. But they calmly said, "You haven't tasted it? Now taste it!" The interrogators cut my clothes with scissors so that they could take them off. My arm was wounded by the scissors. They told me that if I said a thing, they would kill my entire family. I was really injured.[35]

His interrogator whispered in his ear that he would be raped if he did not confess, and then described how it would be done by inserting a bottle in his anus.

In 2002, the special rapporteur on violence against women reported that Soraya Dalaian had been repeatedly raped by two men over a 24-hour period in Evin prison in 1997. She reported that this was not an isolated case and that women prisoners were systematically raped by judges and high-ranking officials. She alleged there were suites available in prisons for that specific purpose.[36]

Canadian Iranian photojournalist Zahra Kazemi was arrested and detained in Evin prison in 2003. She was admitted to the hospital a few days later with extensive injuries, including evidence that she had suffered a "'very brutal rape.'" She died from her injuries.[37] A student activist reported that when he and fellow activists were detained in July 2007, interroga-

---

35. IHRDC, Witness Statement of "Mahdis," at 6, *available at* http://www.iranhrdc.org/english/publications/witness-testimony/3181-witness-statement-mahdis.html.

36. ECOSOC, Commission on Human Rights, *Report of the special Rapporteur on Violence against women, its causes and consequences, Ms. Radhika Coomaraswamy, submitted in accordance with Commission on Human Rights resolution 2000/49, communication to and from Government*, ¶ 49, U.N. Doc. E/CN.4/2002/83/Add.1 (Jan. 28, 2002) [hereinafter Coomaraswamy Report], *available at* http://daccess-dds-ny.un.org/doc/UNDOC/GEN/G02/104/44/PDF/G0210444.pdf.

37. IHRDC, IMPUNITY IN IRAN: THE DEATH OF ZAHRA KAZEMI 7-8 (2006), *available at* http://www.iranhrdc.org/english/publications/reports/3148-impunity-in-iran-the-death-of-photojournalist-zahra-kazemi.html.

tors threatened them with rape with soda bottles or hot eggs in an effort to convince them to confess to serious charges.[38]

Women prisoners were systematically raped by judges and high-ranking officials. She alleged there were suites available in prisons for that specific purpose.

However, Islamic Republic authorities have consistently denied allegations of rape, and failed to address complaints, intervene or protect victims.[39] The United Nations has never received a satisfactory response to its repeated requests for verification of rape allegations. For example, in response to a request for verification of the rape allegations against the religious judge in 1992, the Iranian ambassador stated that the name had not been found in the Ghazvin prison or civil registries. He also reported that there had not been any proven case of torture in Iran in 1990 and 1991.[40] In 2001, the U.N. special representative and the rapporteur on violence against women jointly requested information on Soraya Dalaian's rape allegations. The Islamic Republic responded with the alleged dates of her imprisonment but failed to acknowledge her rape allegations.[41]

In 2009, multiple regime agencies launched investigations into the deplorable conditions, including allegations of sexual abuse and rape, at the Kahrizak Detention Center. While some

---

38. See HUMAN RIGHTS WATCH, YOU CAN DETAIN ANYONE FOR ANYTHING: IRAN'S BROADENING CLAMPDOWN ON INDEPENDENT ACTIVISM 43 (2008).
39. See Secretary-General Note 1990, *supra* note 24, at 4; Galindo Pohl Report 1987, *supra* note 11, at 18-23.
40. Galindo Pohl Report 1992, *supra* note 29, ¶ 359.
41. Coomaraswamy Report, *supra* note 36, ¶ 50; ECOSOC, Commission on Human Rights, *Report on the situation of human rights in the Islamic Republic of Iran, prepared by the Special Representative of the Commission on Human Rights, Mr. Maurice Danby Copithorne,* 31, U.N. Doc. E/CN.4/2002/42 (Jan. 16, 2002), *available at* http://www.unhchr.ch/huridocda/huridoca.nsf/e06a5300f90fa0238025668700518ca4/40fc68cd8a9a97f9c1256b8100525f97/$FILE/G0210126.pdf.

guards and judicial officials were arrested and disciplined,[42] the investigators denied finding any evidence of rape. In December 2009, the *Majlis* special committee to investigate the situation of the detainees of the post-election events issued a report that concluded:

> The Committee members had other investigations and the committee of the Secretariat of the Supreme National Security Council also investigated the matter in detail, and the results of all three committees of the *Majlis*, the judiciary, and the Supreme National Security Council conformed to one another completely, and it is announced that after the comprehensive investigations, we have not gotten to any case of sexual assault and strongly deny that.[43]

Islamic Republic authorities have consistently denied allegations of rape, and failed to address complaints, intervene or protect victims.

II. Prison Rape Violates International and Iranian Law

Although rape is a crime in the Islamic Republic, as noted by the United Nation special rapporteur on violence against women, the evidentiary standards are high and difficult to prove. In 2005, she noted that "[a] victim of rape can only prove her claim by presenting several male witnesses." She described a case where the rape victim was unable to meet this threshold and therefore was charged with adultery.[44] The evidentiary requirements are even more difficult to meet for victims in prison.

42. IHRDC, A YEAR LATER: SUPPRESSION CONTINUES IN IRAN 13 (2010), *available at* http://www.iranhrdc.org/english/publications/reports/3162-a-year-later-suppression-continues-in-iran.html?p=3.
43. VIOLENT AFTERMATH, *supra* note 2, at 48.
44. See ECOSOC, Commission on Human Rights, Report of the Special Rapporteur on violence against women, its causes and consequences, Yakin Erturk, ¶ 56, U.N. Doc. E/CN.u/2006/61/add.3 (Jan. 27, 2006), *available at* http://www.universalhumanrights index.org/documents/848/822/document/en/text.html.

Prison rape constitutes an act of torture, which is absolutely prohibited under both Iranian and international human rights law. Article 38 of the Iranian Constitution provides that "all forms of torture for the purpose of extracting confessions or acquiring information are forbidden."[45] The international prohibition against torture is codified in the Convention Against Torture and Other Cruel, Inhuman or Degrading Treatment or Punishment (CAT).[46] It is also set forth in several other international instruments including Article 7 of the International Covenant on Civil and Political Rights which provides that "no one shall be subjected to torture or to cruel, inhuman or degrading treatment or punishment."[47] While the Islamic Republic has declined to be a party to CAT, its authorities are still obligated to respect the convention's terms as it merely codified the already-existing universal prohibition against torture.[48]

Torture is defined in CAT as

> any act by which severe pain or suffering, whether physical or mental, is intentionally inflicted on a person for such purposes as obtaining from him or a third person information or a confession . . . when such pain or suffering is inflicted by or at the instigation of or with the consent or acquiescence of a public official or other person acting in an official capacity.[49]

---

45. Qanun-i Assasiyih Jumhuriyih Islamiyih Iran [Constitution of the Islamic Republic of Iran] 1358 [adopted 1979, amended 1989], art. 38.

46. Convention Against Torture and Other Cruel, Inhuman or Degrading Treatment or Punishment, GA res. 39/46, annex, 39 UN GAOR Supp. (No. 51) at 197, UN Doc. A/39/51 (1984); 1465 UNTS 85, *available at* aadel.iranhrdc.org [hereinafter Convention Against Torture or CAT].

47. International Covenant on Civil and Political Rights, art. 7, Mar. 23, 1976, 999 U.N.T.S. 171 [hereinafter ICCPR]. Iran signed the ICCPR on April 4, 1968 and ratified the agreement on June 24, 1975 without reservations.

48. See Renee C. Redman, *Defining "Torture": The Collateral Effect on Immigration Law of the Attorney General's Narrow Interpretation of "Specifically Intended" When Applied to United States Interrogators*, 62 N.Y. UNIV. ANNUAL SURVEY OF AM. LAW 465, 470 (2007).

49. Convention Against Torture, *supra* note 46, art. 1.

The U.N. special rapporteurs on torture have consistently noted that rape in prison is torture.[50] For example, the first rapporteur included rape as a method of physical torture in his 1986 report[51] and reiterated his position in 1992:

> Since it was clear that rape or other sexual assaults against woman in detention were a particular ignominious violation of the inherent dignity and the right to physical integrity of the human being, they accordingly constituted an act of torture.[52]

The Committee on Torture, the body charged with monitoring compliance with CAT, has found that rape of detained women by police constitutes torture.[53] The international criminal tribunals for both the former Yugoslavia and Rwanda have also ruled that rape in detention is a form of torture.[54]

---

50. The U.N. Commission on Human Rights first appointed a special Rapporteur to "examine questions relevant to torture" in 1985. In 2008, the mandate was extended for three years. Office of the United Nations High Commissioner on Human Rights, Special Rapporteur on torture and other cruel, inhuman or degrading treatment or punishment, http://www2.ohchr.org/english/issues/torture/rapporteur/index.htm.

51. ECOSOC, Commission on Human Rights, *Report by the Special Rapporteur, Mr. P. Kooijmans*, ¶ 119, U.N. Doc. E/CN.4/1986/15 (Feb. 19, 1986), *available at* http://ap.ohchr.org/documents/E/CHR/report/E-CN_4-1986-15.pdf.

52. ECOSOC, Commission on Human Rights, Summary Record of the 21st Meeting, ¶ 35, U.N. Doc. E/CN.4/1992/SR.21 (Feb. 21, 1992); See also Statement by Manfred Nowak, Special Rapporteur on Torture to the 13th session of the Human Rights Council (Mar. 8, 2010), *available at* http://www.ohchr.org/EN/NewsEvents/Pages/DisplayNews.aspx?NewsID=9918&LangID=E (reiterating that "rape in custody always constitutes torture").

53. See, e.g., *C.T. and K.M. v. Sweden*, CAT/C/37/D/279/2005, U.N. Committee Against Torture, Nov. 17, 2006, *available at* http://www.unhcr.org/refworld/docid/47975b00c.html (finding that repeated rapes of detained woman by Rwandan authorities constituted torture); *V. L. v. Switzerland*, CAT/C/37/D/262/2005, U.N. Committee Against Torture, Nov. 20, 2006, *available at* http://www.unhcr.org/refworld/docid/47975afd21.html (finding that rape by Belarus police constituted torture).

54. See, e.g., Prosecutor v. Kunarac, et al., No. IT-96-23 & It-96-23/1-A, Appeal Chamber Judgment, ¶ 150 (June 12, 2002), *available at* http://www.icty.org/x/cases/kunarac/acjug/en/kun-aj020612e.pdf (stating that "sexual violence necessarily gives rise to severe pain or suffering, whether physical or mental, and in this way justifies its characterization as an act of torture"); Prosecutor v. Akayesu, No. ICTR-96-4-T, Judgment, ¶ 687 (Sept. 2, 1998), *available at* http://www.unictr.org/Portals/0/Case/English/Akayesu/judgement/akay001.pdf (stating that "rape in fact constitutes torture when it is inflicted by or at the instigation of or with the consent or acquiescence of a public official or other person acting in an official capacity").

Periodical and Internet Sources Bibliography

The following articles have been selected to supplement the diverse views presented in this chapter.

Mark Adomanis	"The Prison Rape Scandal in Georgia and the Danger of a 'Morality-Based' Foreign Policy," *Forbes*, September 25, 2012.
Kate Allen	"Rape in Iran's Prisons: The Cruellest Torture," *Telegraph*, November 1, 2010.
Mariano Castillo	"Report: Women Targeted in Sexual Violence as Colombian Forces Battle Rebels," CNN, September 21, 2011.
Matthew Chance	"Former Georgia Prison Guard: I Witnessed Abuse for Years," CNN, September 23, 2012.
Saeed Kamali Dehghan	"Iran Giving Out Condoms for Criminals to Rape Us, Say Jailed Activists," *Guardian*, June 24, 2011.
Maria Neophytou	"Sexual Violence and War: Inevitable?," openDemocracy, May 19, 2011. http://www.opendemocracy.net/5050 /maria-neophytou/sexual-violence-and -war-inevitable.
Stewart M. Patrick	"Stopping Wartime Sexual Abuse—Of Men," *Atlantic*, July 20, 2011.
Charlotte Rachael Proudman	"War Rape: The Forgotten Pandemic Sweeping Syria," *Independent*, January 21, 2013.
Lara Stemple	"The Hidden Victims of Wartime Rape," *New York Times*, March 1, 2011.
Eric Westervelt	"Silence Broken on Red Army Rapes in Germany," NPR, July 17 2009.

For Further Discussion

Chapter 1

1. What similarities are there in attitudes toward rape in the various countries discussed in this chapter? How do these similarities in attitudes make it difficult to prevent or punish rape?

2. Andrew Solomon discusses the writing of Susan Brownmiller, who argued that rape was a common result of power differentials between men and women. Do the viewpoints in this chapter support that argument? Explain your answer citing specific evidence from the pieces you have read.

Chapter 2

1. Are there any examples of systemic child abuse among the viewpoints in this chapter? Does systemic abuse require different responses than isolated incidents of abuse? Explain.

2. Considering the other viewpoints you have read in the first and second chapters, what factors might slow the United Nations' efforts to prevent peacekeepers from committing sexual violence against children?

Chapter 3

1. Based on the viewpoints by Amelia Gentleman and Nathalie Rothschild, do you think the threat of trafficking in Europe and Britain is overstated? Explain your reasoning using specific evidence from the two viewpoints.

2. Based on the viewpoints in this chapter, does migrating make people more vulnerable to sexual violence, or do

they migrate because they are vulnerable? Explain your answer using evidence from the viewpoints.

Chapter 4

1. Based on the viewpoints in this chapter, why is sexual violence often used in armed conflict? Explain your answer.

2. Prison rape often reflects a political culture of authoritarianism and violence. Does that seem to apply to prison rape in Iran as discussed by the Iran Human Rights Documentation Center? Explain your answer.

Organizations to Contact

The editors have compiled the following list of organizations concerned with the issues debated in this book. The descriptions are derived from materials provided by the organizations. All have publications or information available for interested readers. The list was compiled on the date of publication of the present volume; the information provided here may change. Be aware that many organizations take several weeks or longer to respond to inquiries, so allow as much time as possible.

ACT for Kids
210 West Sprague Avenue, Spokane, WA   99201
(866) 348-5437 • fax: (509) 747-0609
e-mail: resources@actforkids.org
website: www.actforkids.org

ACT for Kids is a nonprofit organization that provides resources, consultation, research, and training for the prevention and treatment of child abuse and sexual violence. The organization publishes workbooks, manuals, and books such as *He Told Me Not to Tell* and *How to Survive the Sexual Abuse of Your Child*.

Amnesty International
5 Penn Plaza, 14th floor, New York, NY   10001
(212) 807-8400 • fax: (212) 463-9193
e-mail: aimember@aiusa.org
website: www.amnestyusa.org

Amnesty International is a worldwide movement of people who campaign for internationally recognized human rights. Its vision is of a world in which every person enjoys all of the human rights enshrined in the Universal Declaration of Human Rights and other international human rights standards. Each year it publishes a report on its work and its concerns throughout the world. Amnesty International highlights sexual violence as a human rights abuse in many articles and reports available through its website, such as "Bosnia and Herzegovina: Time for Republika Srpska to Make Reparations for War-Time Rape" and "Global Campaign Targets Rape in Conflict Zones."

Association for the Rights of Catholics in the Church (ARCC)

3150 Newgate Drive, Florissant, MO   63033
(870) 235-5200
website: www.arcc-catholic-rights.net

Founded in 1980 by lay and clerical Catholics, the Association for the Rights of Catholics in the Church's (ARCC's) primary goal is to promote accountability, institutionalize shared decision making, and preserve the rights of all Catholics. On its website, ARCC provides access to archives of its newsletter, variously named *ARCC Light, ARCC Spotlight*, and *ARCC News*. It also includes articles and documents about Catholicism, reform, and sexual abuse within the church.

Centre to End All Sexual Exploitation (CEASE)

PO Box 11471, Edmonton, Alberta   T5J 3K6
    Canada
(780) 471-6143 • fax: (780) 471-6237
e-mail: director@ceasenow.org
website: www.ceasenow.org

The Centre to End All Sexual Exploitation (CEASE) works to address sexual exploitation and the harms created by prostitution through public education, client support, counseling, and emergency poverty relief for individuals recovering from trauma and exploitation. Its website includes reports and articles on the effects of sexual exploitation and trafficking.

Human Rights Watch (HRW)

350 Fifth Avenue, 34th Floor, New York, NY   10118-3299
(212) 290-4700

e-mail: hrwnyc@hrw.org
website: www.hrw.org

Founded in 1978, Human Rights Watch (HRW) is a nongovernmental organization that conducts systematic investigations of human rights abuses in countries around the world. It highlights sexual violence as a human rights abuse, during both peacetime and in conflict situations. HRW publishes many books and reports, as well as annual reports and articles, such as "US: Sexual Violence, Harassment of Immigrant Farmworkers" and "Syria: Sexual Assault in Detention."

Just Detention International (JDI)

3325 Wilshire Boulevard, Suite 340, Los Angeles, CA   90010
(213) 384-1400 • fax: (213) 384-141
e-mail: info@justdetention.org
website: www.justdetention.org

Just Detention International (JDI) is a health and human rights organization that seeks to end sexual abuse in all forms of detention. JDI works to hold government officials accountable for prison rape, promote public support for the safety of prisoners, and provide survivors of violence with access to help. Its website includes fact sheets, reports, and updates relating to sexual violence in prison.

Physicians for Human Rights (PHR)

1156 Fifteenth Street NW, Suite 1001, Washington, DC   20005
(202) 728-5335 • fax: (202) 728-3053
website: http://physiciansforhumanrights.org

Physicians for Human Rights (PHR) is an independent organization that uses medicine and science to stop mass atrocities and human rights violations against individuals. It uses its investigations and expertise to advocate for the protection of human rights victims and the prosecution of those who violate human rights. One of the issues PHR focuses on is rape in wartime, and its website includes background information and reports such as "The Use of Rape as a Weapon of War in Darfur, Sudan" and "Hidden Deaths of Libyan Rape Survivors."

Rape, Abuse, and Incest National Network (RAINN)
1220 L Street NW, Suite 505, Washington, DC   20005
(202) 544-1034
e-mail: info@rainn.org
website: www.rainn.org

Rape, Abuse, and Incest National Network (RAINN) is America's largest anti–sexual violence organization. It created and operates the National Sexual Assault Hotline in conjunction with more than eleven hundred local rape crisis centers. It also carries out programs to prevent sexual violence, help victims, and ensure that rapists are brought to justice. Its website includes news, press releases, and newsletters, as well as numerous resources for victims and information about rape and abuse.

Sex Workers Project
Urban Justice Center, 123 William Street, 16th Floor
New York, NY   10038
(646) 602-5617
e-mail: swp@urbanjustice.org
website: www.sexworkersproject.org

The Sex Workers Project provides client-centered legal and social services to individuals who engage in sex work, regardless of whether they do so by choice, circumstance, or coercion. One of the first programs in the nation to assist survivors of human trafficking, the Sex Workers Project has pioneered an approach to service grounded in human rights, harm reduction, and in the real-life experiences of clients. The project provides legal education workshops for sex workers and training for service providers. It also engages in media advocacy, supports sex worker–led organizing, and conducts human rights documentation of the experiences of sex workers and the survivors of trafficking. Its website includes numerous reports, such as "Use of Raids to Fight Trafficking" and "Behind Closed Doors," about indoor prostitution in New York City.

United Nations Children's Fund (UNICEF)
125 Maiden Lane, New York, NY   10038
(212) 326-7000 • fax: (212) 887-7465
website: www.unicef.org

The United Nations Children's Fund (UNICEF) works to help build a world where the rights of every child are realized. UNICEF works to prevent sexual violence against children and sexual exploitation of children, both in peacetime and in conflict situations. Its website includes numerous articles and reports on sexual violence against children, such as "Caring for Child Survivors of Sexual Abuse" and "Mental Health and Psychosocial Support for Conflict-Related Sexual Violence."

Bibliography of Books

Laura Maria Agustín	*Sex at the Margins: Migration, Labour Markets and the Rescue Industry.* New York: Zed Books, 2007.
Maria Eriksson Baaz and Maria Stern	*Sexual Violence as a Weapon of War?: Perceptions, Prescriptions, Problems in the Congo and Beyond.* New York: Zed Books, 2013.
Paul J. Bailey	*Women and Gender in Twentieth-Century China.* London, UK: Palgrave Macmillan, 2012.
Susan Brownmiller	*Against Our Will: Men, Women and Rape.* New York: Fawcett Columbine, 1993.
Kristin Bumiller	*In an Abusive State: How Neoliberalism Appropriated the Feminist Movement Against Sexual Violence.* Durham, NC: Duke University Press, 2008.
Catherine Burns	*Sexual Violence and the Law in Japan.* New York: RoutledgeCurzon, 2004.
Anne-Marie de Brouwer, Renée Römkens, Charlotte Ku, and Larissa van den Herik, eds.	*Sexual Violence as an International Crime: Interdisciplinary Approaches.* Cambridge, UK: Intersentia, 2012.
Rosa-Linda Fregoso and Cynthia Bejarano, eds.	*Terrorizing Women: Feminicide in the Américas.* Durham, NC: Duke University Press, 2010.

Sorcha Gunne and Zöe Brigley Thompson, eds.	*Feminism, Literature and Rape Narratives: Violence and Violation.* New York: Routledge, 2010.
Sonja M. Hedgepeth and Rochelle G. Saidel, eds.	*Sexual Violence Against Jewish Women During the Holocaust.* Waltham, MA: Brandeis University Press, 2010.
Nicola Henry	*War and Rape: Law, Memory, and Justice.* New York: Routledge, 2011.
Valerie M. Hudson, Bonnie Ballif-Spanvill, Mary Caprioli, and Chad F. Emmett	*Sex and World Peace.* New York: Columbia University Press, 2012.
Mic Hunter	*Honor Betrayed: Sexual Abuse in America's Military.* Fort Lee, NJ: Barricade Books, 2007.
Siddharth Kara	*Sex Trafficking: Inside the Business of Modern Slavery.* New York: Columbia University Press, 2009.
Marie Keenan	*Child Sexual Abuse and the Catholic Church: Gender, Power, and Organizational Culture.* New York: Oxford University Press, 2011.
Janie L. Leatherman	*Sexual Violence and Armed Conflict.* Malden, MA: Polity Press, 2011.
Clare McGlynn and Vanessa E. Munro, eds.	*Rethinking Rape Law: International and Comparative Perspectives.* New York: Routledge, 2010.

Sally Engle Merry   *Gender Violence: A Cultural Perspective.* Malden, MA: Wiley-Blackwell, 2009.

Sally Engle Merry   *Human Rights and Gender Violence: Translating International Law into Local Justice.* Chicago, IL: University of Chicago Press, 2006.

Padmini Murthy and Clyde Lanford Smith, eds.   *Women's Global Health and Human Rights.* Sudbury, MA: Jones and Bartlett Publishers, 2010.

Thomas G. Plante and Kathleen L. McChesney, eds.   *Sexual Abuse in the Catholic Church: A Decade of Crisis, 2002–2012.* Santa Barbara, CA: Praeger, 2011.

Louise Shelley   *Human Trafficking: A Global Perspective.* New York: Cambridge University Press, 2010.

C. Sarah Soh   *The Comfort Women: Sexual Violence and Postcolonial Memory in Korea and Japan.* Chicago, IL: University of Chicago Press, 2008.

Jacqui True   *The Political Economy of Violence Against Women.* New York: Oxford University Press, 2012.

Janet I. Warren and Shelly L. Jackson   *Risk Markers for Sexual Victimization and Predation in Prisons.* New York: Routledge, 2013.

Index

Geographic headings and page numbers in **boldface** refer to viewpoints about that country or region.

C

D